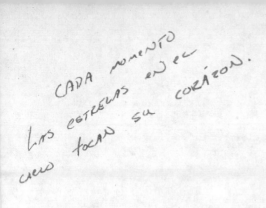

CADA momento
Las estrellas en el
cielo tocan su corazón.

F

THE
HAIKU
ANTHOLOGY

Haiku
and
Senryu
in
English

Edited by
COR VAN DEN HEUVEL

A Fireside Book
Published by Simon & Schuster, Inc.
New York

A Fireside Book,

Published by Simon & Schuster, Inc.

Simon & Schuster Building

Rockefeller Center

1230 Avenue of the Americas

New York, New York 10020

This is a revised edition of a book originally published in 1974

by Doubleday & Co., Inc.

FIRESIDE and colophon are registered trademarks

of Simon & Schuster, Inc.

Designed by Barbara Marks

Manufactured in the United States of America

10 9 8 7 6 5 4 3

Library of Congress Cataloging in Publication Data

Van den Heuvel, Cor, date.
  The haiku anthology.
  "A Fireside book."
  1. Haiku, American.   2. Haiku, Canadian.
3. Senryu, American.   4. Senryu, Canadian.
I. Title.
PS593.H3V3   1986   811'.04'08   86-11886
ISBN: 0-671-62837-2

The editor thanks the following poets, magazines, and publishers for permission to print these poems:

  (Abbreviations: AH: *American Haiku;* BLP: Burnt Lake Press; BS: *Brussels Sprout;* CI: *Cicada;* DR: *Dragonfly;* FHP: From Here Press; FR: *Frogpond;* HC: *High/Coo;* HH: *Haiku Highlights;* HM: *Haiku Magazine;* HSA: Haiku Society of America, Inc.; HW: *Haiku West;* MH: *Modern Haiku;* NWH: *New World Haiku;* SO: *Seer Ox;* WC: *Wind Chimes;* 1/1: Vol. 1, No. 1. A *P* after a magazine's abbreviation indicates the press associated with it; if the address of a press is not mentioned below, it may be found in the Book List on p. 22.)

(Note: Every effort has been made to contact copyright holders; the editor would
  be pleased to hear from any copyright holders not acknowledged below.)

Helen C. Acton: "Beads of spring rain" from WC 9, copyright 1983 by WC; by
  permission of the author.
Eric Amann: all 7 poems from *Cicada Voices: Selected Haiku of Eric Amann
  1966–1979,* edited by George Swede, HCP, © by Eric Amann 1983; by permis-
  sion of the author.
Nick Avis: "freshly fallen snow" and "the evening star" from WC 8, copyright ©
  1983 by Hal Roth; by permission of the author.
Bob Boldman: "Sitting" from *My Lord's Necklace,* Portals Press, Bellingham, WA,
  copyright © 1980 Robert Boldman; "day darkens" and "a moment" from CI
  5/1, © CI 1981; "a fin" from BS II/4, © copyright 1982 by Alexis Kaye
  Rotella; "I read" from BS II/3, © copyright 1982 by Alexis Kaye Rotella;
  "walking," "the priest" and "in the temple" from *Walking With the River,* HCP,
  © 1980 by Bob Boldman; "I end" and "touching" from CI 5/4, © CI 1981; "in
  the heat" from WC 6, copyright © 1982 by Hal Roth; "in the doll's" from
  MH XIII/1, copyright 1982 Robert Spiess; "mist" from BS I/2, © 1981 by
  Alexis Rotella; "face" from WC 7, copyright © 1983 by Hal Roth; "JANUARY
  FIRST" from BS I/3, © 1981 BS; "leaves" from CI 4/4, © CI 1980; "i ham-
  mer" from *Eating A Melon,* WCP, copyright 1981 by Robert Boldman; "just
  past sunset" from FR II/2, copyright © 1979 HSA; by permission of the
  author.

(*continued on page 362*)

To Harold G. Henderson and R. H. Blyth

The editor would like to thank the poets for their co-operation in putting together this book, artist Kimio Take-yama for the artwork on the cover, Fireside Books editor Tim McGinnis for helping turn it into a reality, and Leigh Larrecq van den Heuvel for her advice and encouragement when it looked as though it might never be more than a dream.

CONTENTS

A NOTE ON THE SELECTION AND
LAYOUT OF THE POEMS

Selection: Some readers may wonder why I've chosen certain poems in this book which are, on the surface, similar to others. If a haiku is a good one, it doesn't matter if the subject has been used before. The writing of variations on certain subjects in haiku, sometimes using the same or similar phrases (or even changing a few words of a previous haiku), is one of the most interesting challenges it offers a poet, and can result in refreshingly different ways of "seeing anew" for the reader. This is an aspect of traditional Japanese haiku which is hard for many Westerners, with their ideas of uniqueness and Romantic individualism, to accept. But some of the most original voices in haiku do not hesitate to dare seeming derivative if they see a way of reworking an "old" image.

Layout: Due to the fact that the words of a haiku provide only the bare essentials of the image, with which the reader's awareness works to create the haiku moment, it is important that the reader is not distracted from those essentials. The layout of the page, the amount of white space within which the words may work, and the choice of the other haiku on the spread all play a role in determining how the reader will direct his attention. Such considerations have been second only to the selection of the haiku themselves in the editing of this book.

PREFACE TO THE SECOND EDITION

Someone, probably thinking of Bashō's famous haiku about the-sound-of-a-frog-jumping-into-an-old-pond, once likened the English language haiku movement to a small puddle far from the mainstream of poetry. If so, the puddle is doing very well on its own. While the mainstream moves, for the most part, sluggishly through gray fogs of obscurity and intellectualization, the puddle is ablaze with color and light—as a glance through this book will show.

There are no signs of its ever drying up—on the contrary, it seems to be spring-fed—and the "frogs" who inhabit it are singing songs filled with original imagery, stark beauty, sparkling wit, intense emotion, peaceful calm, and acute awareness.

This edition of *The Haiku Anthology* contains around 700 haiku, senryu, and related works—about 500 more than there were in the first edition, which was published in the spring of 1974. Extraordinary things have happened to haiku since then—due, primarily, to the innovative, fresh approaches brought to the genre by the poets represented in this book. Haiku will become what the poets make it, to paraphrase the late Harold G. Henderson,[1] and our haiku literature is as rich and varied as it is because such poets as Anita Virgil, Alan Pizzarelli, Michael McClintock, Marlene Mountain, George Swede, Raymond Roseliep, John Wills, Gary Hotham, Alexis Rotella, and others have led the way into directions of accomplishment undreamed of in the early years of the movement.

These accomplishments are also, indirectly, the result of work by scholars and translators of Japanese literature, such as Henderson himself. In recent years new books by Makoto

---

[1] One of the pioneer scholar/translators of haiku, Harold Henderson died in 1974, shortly after the first edition of the *Anthology* was published.

Ueda, Earl Miner, Hiroaki Sato, Burton Watson, and Donald Keene have deepened our understanding of Japanese haiku and its related genres, significantly affecting how we write their counterparts in English. (See the Book List following this Preface.)

In the years between editions there have been three major developments: the emergence of the one-liner as a common form for haiku and senryu; the growing practice of writing longer works, such as sequences and renga; and the increasing importance of human relationships, especially sex and love, as subject matter. (See Appendix B for definitions of haiku, senryu, renga, and related terms.)

Though many poets had been moving toward more freedom for the haiku form in the early seventies, especially away from the restrictions of the 5-7-5 syllable count, it was only in the latter half of the decade that the one-line form became more than an occasional exception to the three-line "rule." The three-line form, with no set syllable count, remains the standard, but some of the best haiku in English have been written in one line, and the form is now widely used.[2]

Three people were initially responsible for gaining its general acceptance: Marlene Mountain (formerly known as Marlene Wills) was the first to write good one-line haiku with some regularity; Hiroaki Sato translated Japanese haiku into one-liners and lent "legitimacy" to the writing of original one-liners in English;[3] and Matsuo Allard furthered the cause of the one-liner by writing polemical essays in its favor, edit-

[2] The first edition had only a single one-liner, Michael Segers' "in the eggshell."

[3] Sato's one-line haiku translations started appearing in magazines in 1976, and over 600 are in the anthology *From the Country of Eight Islands* (1981). Sato also lent confirmation to an earlier conclusion by William J. Higginson, which appeared in a small book called *Itadakimasu* in 1971, that 10 to 14 syllables in English, rather than 17, most closely approximates the sound length of the 17 *onji* in a traditional Japanese haiku.

10

ing and publishing several short-lived but important magazines devoted to it, publishing chapbooks of them, and by writing them himself.[4]

The most common argument for one-liners is that the Japanese write haiku in one vertical line or column and therefore we should write in one line also, but of course horizontally in the Western style. Strict "three-liner" advocates argue that since the Japanese haiku breaks into three parts because of the 5-7-5 syllable (*onji*) form—patterns that occur naturally in the Japanese language—the only way to parallel it in English is to write in three lines. Of course many poets write in one form or the other simply because they think the particular poem they are writing works better in that form.

There has also been some experimentation with two-line haiku—Bob Boldman has probably had the most success with them—but they are still quite rare. A few poets have tried writing English language tanka. These five-line poems have usually been most successful when done in the introspective style of Takuboku Ishikawa (1885–1912) rather than in the traditional lyric manner—for example the tanka of Bob Boldman and Michael McClintock on pages 40 and 140-141.

Longer forms in the shape of sequences have been a part of the haiku scene since at least the sixties and a few short ones were included in the first edition, but they have increased in popularity in recent years. While most sequences have been made up of haiku or senryu which can stand alone as poems themselves—at least their authors intended them to have that ability—Marlene Mountain and Alexis Rotella have written a kind in which the individual elements, though firmly rooted in haiku and senryu, depend largely on their context for their effectiveness, and only one or two out of several may be able to stand alone. (See Appendix A for examples.) Similar se-

[4] Matsuo Allard's press was first called Sun-Lotus and later became The First Haiku Press. As far as can be determined, the press is no longer in existence. Matsuo Allard also used the name R. Clarence Matsuo-Allard.

quences of haiku or tanka that depend on context for meaning have been written in Japanese. They are called rensaku.

An attempt at English language renga was published as early as 1968 in *Haiku Magazine,* but it wasn't till the midseventies that the form became of any importance. Also called "linked-verse poem" or "renku," renga were originally written at a live session, like a jazz improvisation, but in English have most often been done through the mails, with two, three, or more poets writing links in turn.

William J. Higginson and Tadashi Kondo played seminal roles in awakening interest in renga early in 1976 with discussions at the Haiku Society of America. These were recorded in the society's newsletter, and later that year *Haiku Magazine* put out an issue devoted to renga and haibun (prose pieces written in the spirit of haiku). In the late seventies and early eighties, Marlene Mountain and Hiroaki Sato participated in a number of renga that appeared in *Cicada* and in the Haiku Society's *Frogpond*. Sato, one of the most influential figures in the haiku movement in recent years (he was president of the Haiku Society of America for three years, 1979–81), has not, as far as I know, published any individual haiku or senryu. The one included in this book is the hokku, or starting verse, from one of his solo renga. His book *One Hundred Frogs: From Renga to Haiku to English* (1983) gives an informative and entertaining history of Japanese renga, along with a brief account of English language renga and a small anthology of the latter. In Japan haiku originated when the hokku of *haikai no renga* began to be written as an independent poem. The process has been reversed in the West. Renga developed here when haiku poets started looking for ways to extend the haiku into longer forms. Its importance for this anthology is that the practice of writing renga has helped stimulate innovation in the writing of haiku and senryu and has encouraged the exchange of ideas and a sense of community among poets by bringing them in closer contact with one another. (See Appendix A for an example of English language renga along with more information on how they are written.)

Another longer form is the haibun. These prose pieces—which usually contain one or more haiku—have been tried occasionally in English but except for some parts of two novels by Jack Kerouac little of significance has appeared yet. In several passages in *Desolation Angels* and *The Dharma Bums,* Kerouac has come closer than any other writer in English to the terse, elliptical, nature-inspired prose that characterizes the genre. His descriptions of his experiences alone on Desolation Mountain have the whirling brevity and vivid immediacy of some of Bashō's great haibun. Unfortunately, the few haiku he includes are not of comparable merit.

The last major development involves subject matter. Though there were a few haiku or senryu in the first edition dealing with sex—some of Michael McClintock's come immediately to mind—they were rare exceptions. Sex, love, and the whole range of human emotions and relationships have now become fairly common themes. Rod Willmot, one of the movement's most important critics and one of Canada's leading haiku poets, calls most of these poems "psychological haiku"; those specifically about sex he has called "erotic haiku." "Serious senryu" would be more accurate, I think, for most of them. Instead of recreating a moment of awareness in which human nature is related to nature, they give us a moment of awareness about one's own inner feelings or one's relationships with other human beings.

Senryu began as comic verse, but that does not mean it has to be called haiku when it becomes serious. It seems useful to me to keep the two genres distinct in somewhat the same way the Japanese do—haiku relates to nature and the seasons, senryu relates to human nature. Traditionally, the Japanese have ensured this by insisting that to be a haiku the poem must have a season word (*kigo*), while a senryu does not. They have always had the same form. It is the subject matter that determines the genre—not the form, and not whether the subject matter is looked at humorously or not. Haiku itself began as a kind of humorous verse, and one can still write a funny haiku.

In recent years more and more writers have been creating comic and serious senryu that rival the best haiku in the depth of insight they reveal and the emotional richness they convey. Michael McClintock, who edited a magazine (*seer ox*) in the mid-seventies devoted to senryu, and Alan Pizzarelli, who wrote many comic senryu about the same time, were probably the first to spark significant interest in the genre—though Clement Hoyt and a few others had written fine senryu earlier. Recently George Swede, a Canadian, has become one of the best senryu writers in English—of both the humorous and serious kinds. He is a highly original writer of haiku as well, and his work in both genres has influenced a number of other poets. In the United States, Marlene Mountain (particularly in her sequences), Alexis Rotella, and Bob Boldman—among others—have led the way in bringing psychology, or more subjectivity, into both haiku and senryu. Rotella has polished this facet of the art with such brilliance that she has become in only a few years one of the stars in the growing constellation of outstanding haiku/senryu poets. (For critical estimates of her work, see Appendix A.)

As in the first edition, I have not tried to separate the senryu from the haiku in this book. Not because of the slight difficulty in deciding which is which, for a few do overlap, but because an interesting variety, contrast, and resonance can result from their juxtaposition.

Though one-liners, longer works, and serious senryu are the most obvious, widespread developments, there have been many other successful explorations of the possibilities of haiku and its related genres. Usually these have been accomplished by the individual genius, or style, of a particular poet, from the minimalist and "unaloud" pieces of Marlene Mountain to the extended haiku and "sound" poems of Pizzarelli. Mountain had published little in the haiku magazines before exploding on the scene in 1976 with her book, *the old tin roof*. Since then she has figured prominently in the movement, and her inventive and powerful writing has helped to shape many of the changes that have taken place. Though Pizzarelli had a few poems in the first edition of the anthology, he has since become the clown/magician of the haiku world, materializing an amazing array of word-wonders that brings the wise craziness of the poet/monks of the past into the modern world of chrome and neon.

Raymond Roseliep, another sui-generis poet, had tried his hand at haiku in the early seventies, but his main work and reputation then was in traditionally Western genres. When he later devoted his craft to haiku he kept a Western flavor in it which makes it hard to say exactly what his marvelously witty and off-the-wall creations are—William J. Higginson has resorted to the word "liepku." One of the most prolific poets in the movement, Roseliep left us a large body of these sparkling and delightful poems which undeniably belong to haiku/senryu before he died in 1983.

In fact, all the voices in this book have unique qualities: Gary Hotham is a master of what might be called the "plain," or "subtle" haiku, so ordinary that unless you are especially alert you may miss the resonance stirring beneath the simple image of, say, an overdue book or a paper cup; Martin Shea has a dramatist's skill in setting a scene that tells a story—his images lead us into a narrative that continues on in our minds after the poem is read; Penny Harter zooms in for close-ups of a cat's whisker or the toe of a boot with such startling clarity and effective cropping they loom into a sudden indefinable significance; Scott Montgomery's work often has a surreal, dreamlike aura about it; Arizona Zipper has a wry, earthy, down-home humor; and so on.

Canadian poets have long played an important role in the English language haiku movement, especially Eric Amann, who edited *Haiku* and *Cicada,* perhaps English language haiku's most influential magazines.[5] They are still unsurpassed for excellence in both content and design, though both have ceased publication—the last, *Cicada,* in 1981. Amann and Rod Willmot, both of whom were in the first edition, and George Swede are Canada's leading haiku poets. Among the other new voices from the Canadian part of the "puddle," LeRoy Gorman's and Chuck Brickley's are perhaps the brightest. The movement has branches overseas as well, and included in this collection are haiku by an Australian, Jan Bostok, and by the Japanese poet Tadashi Kondo, who writes haiku in both Japanese and English.

All the major American figures in the first edition appear again in this one—including Foster Jewell, J. W. Hackett, Nicholas Virgilio, Robert Spiess, John Wills, Michael McClintock, William J. Higginson, Anita Virgil, and O. Mabson Southard (then writing under the name Mabelsson Norway). Several of these poets have been very active in the haiku movement in the years between editions. Michael McClintock was especially busy in the mid-seventies with his Seer Ox press—putting out the magazine and several chapbooks by various poets, while also writing and publishing work of his own. Robert Spiess took over the editorship of *Modern Haiku* magazine in 1978 (from Kay Mormino, who started it in 1969), keeping it the stable, smooth-sailing, general arbiter of the haiku scene it had always been—where the conservatives and radicals of the movement can both be heard but moderation predominates. His poetry has taken on a darker tone in recent years, yet it still glows with keenly perceived moments from the world of forest and stream.

William J. Higginson was a sort of guru to the haiku

[5] Two important anthologies of Canadian haiku have appeared: George Swede's *Canadian Haiku Anthology* (1979) and *Haïku: Anthologie canadienne/Canadian Anthology* (1985), edited by Dorothy Howard and André Duhaime, a bilingual collection of French language and English language haiku.

movement in the early and mid-seventies. He left the puddle for a time, but became active there again in the eighties. He and Willmot are probably our most astute critics. As well as being a critic/poet Higginson is a scholar/translator of Japanese literature. In his recent *The Haiku Handbook: How to Write, Share, and Teach Haiku* (1985) he gives one of the clearest delineations of what a haiku does and how it does it that exists in English. He also presents a comprehensive picture of the development of both Japanese and world haiku from its beginnings to the present, succinctly condensing and incorporating with his own translations, research, and analyses the most important new information about haiku and its related genres from the large body of scholarly works on Japanese literature of the past twenty-five years. It is an indispensable companion volume to the great works of Blyth and Henderson.

Nicholas Virgilio's work continues to illuminate the shadows of death. Adding to the elegiac series of haiku about his brother, who died in Vietnam, he has created a moving testament to the power of art and love to rescue the memory of a loved one from the blankness of death. The autumn wind, which somehow evokes trust and fear at the same time, blows through his haiku with a strange consolatory power that is unforgettable.

"A reclusive and fiercely independent spirit," J. W. Hackett has not been directly involved with the haiku movement since the sixties, when his work appeared in the haiku magazines, but his haiku continue to attract new readers and writers to the genre. They are probably better known than those of any other non-Japanese poet, and have been praised by R. H. Blyth, Alan Watts, and Jack Kerouac. However, for more than a decade now he has been mainly interested in writing longer poems, a number of which are in *The Zen Haiku and Other Zen Poems of J. W. Hackett* (1983), a book that, happily, also contains all the haiku from his long-popular *The Way of Haiku*.

Between 1974 and 1980, Foster Jewell produced nine more of his enchanting chapbooks of haiku, two of them in collaboration with his wife, Rhoda de Long Jewell. While evoking vivid images of the woodlands, mountains, and deserts he loved, Jewell also had a way of summoning the spirit of nature into his haiku so that you felt its presence—in the sound of thunder along a beach or in the silence of a moonrise. In 1984 he passed away into the silences he wrote so intimately about.

O. Mabson Southard remains a mysterious figure, like his changing name, and much to the regret of the many admirers of his haiku there has been no new work by him in the haiku magazines for several years now. He has, it is said, recently turned his mind to other concerns, including the study of mathematics. The sharp clarity and depth of his images—the rocks and tree coming out of the mist in his well-known "old rooster" haiku, the loon's cry crossing the still lake, the sparrow knocking snow from a fence-rail, the dogwood petal carrying its moonlight into the darkness—these and many more will ensure that his name (or names) will endure as long as there are readers of haiku.

Anita Virgil's stature, like Southard's, becomes more ensured as we see how her haiku continue to shine as brightly as ever though the years go by: the flickering light on the pine bark, that feeling of sinking through the snow-crust, the spring peepers, the shadows on the dinner plates. Virgil, too, was silent for a few years but in the early eighties started writing again. One of the first of these new haiku was "holding you." It won first prize in a special erotic-haiku contest conducted by *Cicada* that resulted in the book *Erotic Haiku* (1983), edited by Rod Willmot.

John Wills has been one of the most productive poets in the movement—especially in the years since the last edition—and he has found a way of haiku that is closer to nature, more resonant with its mystery and wonder, than the work of perhaps anyone else writing today in whatever genre. With only a few syllables, he creates haiku of such clarity and purity they seem to have come from the hand of nature itself. A critical appraisal of Wills' haiku appears in Appendix A. (For short biographical notes on all the poets see Appendix C.)

There are some poets in this book that should have been in the earlier edition but were not. Jack Kerouac, for example. He was one of the first to write haiku in English, and to do so in a distinctively modern, American style, using a colloquial idiom and everyday, local images rather than turning out imitation Japanese poems about cherry blossoms.

The medium for the writers of haiku in English has continued to be the haiku magazines and the small presses that publish haiku chapbooks. They are the movement. *Leanfrog,* a haiku newsletter published on the West Coast, listed nineteen magazines in 1982 that were accepting haiku, with many of them specializing exclusively in haiku literature. In addition, it listed seven haiku societies. The haiku magazines come and go like most small-press ventures, but a few have managed to publish for several years. The most important magazines and presses still publishing are included in the Book List.

After about twenty-five years of English language haiku do we know what a haiku is? There seems to be no general consensus—which may be a sign of its health and vitality. There is still much talk about awareness and perception—less about Zen and the Infinite. Hiroaki Sato, especially, has tried to get the Zen out of haiku, saying that Western critics have been responsible for the association and that Japanese haiku poets have much simpler intentions than to try to give their readers "enlightenment." "Haiku have been written," he writes, "to congratulate, to praise, to describe, to express gratitude, wit, cleverness, disappointment, resentment, or what have you, but rarely to convey enlightenment" (*One Hundred Frogs,* p. 131).

It is said that Bashō toward the end of his life felt his love for haiku might be a worldly attachment standing in the way of self-realization—but, try as he would, he could not give it up. What did haiku give him that made it so hard to abandon—even for the promise of spiritual peace? It must have been more than just the opportunity to express gratitude or resentment, or the chance to congratulate or describe. His disciple Dohō's explanation of what the Master meant by his famous saying "Learn about a pine tree from a pine tree, and about a bamboo plant from a bamboo plant" suggests an answer:

> What he meant was that a poet should detach the mind from his own personal self. Nevertheless some poets interpret the word "learn" in their own ways and never really "learn." For "learn" means to enter into the object, perceive its delicate life and feel its feelings, whereupon a poem forms itself. A lucid description of the object is not enough; unless the poem contains feelings which have spontaneously emerged from the object, it will show the object and the poet's self as two separate entities, making it impossible to attain a true poetic sentiment. The poem will be artificial, for it is composed by the poet's personal self.[6]

Now Dohō is not explaining enlightenment, but neither is he explaining how to "praise" or "describe"—in fact, he states that description is not enough. The process he does set forth, however, sounds very similar to the way Zen Buddhists describe the path to enlightenment: achieving detachment from the self, becoming one with existence. If you become one with something other than yourself, leaving self behind, isn't that a way to know, or to at least catch a glimpse of, the truth that all existence is one? If that's not enlightenment, it certainly seems like a step in the right direction. Of course, true enlightenment is said to require giving up *all* attachments—

[6] From Makoto Ueda's *Matsuo Bashō,* pp. 167-168.

so the monk must also give up those things that have helped him along the way, including his koans, his sitting, and even his desire for enlightenment itself. So because a Buddhist poet feels he must give up poetry doesn't necessarily mean that the poetry wasn't useful along the way. R. H. Blyth has written:

> A haiku is the expression of a temporary en-
> lightenment, in which we see into the life of
> things. . . . It is a way in which the cold
> winter rain, the swallows of evening, even the
> very day in its hotness, and the length of the
> night become truly alive, share in our hu-
> manity, speak their own silent and expressive
> language.[7]

Since writing the passage quoted earlier, Sato seems to have taken a new look at this question. In a talk called "Bashō and the Concept of 'The Way' in Japanese Poetry," given to the Haiku Society of America in December 1983, he quoted Bashō as saying that "poetry writing is another vehicle for entering the True Way (*makoto no michi*)," and pointed out that the "True Way" means Buddhism. Bashō, who "trained in Zen," apparently felt, at least part of the time, that he was on a spiritual path when he wrote haiku.[8]

Ultimately haiku eludes definition. It is "always evolving, burgeoning, growing," Rod Willmot writes in a recent letter— and it may be a good thing, he adds, if, rather than working toward a restrictive definition, we continue in our present direction, where haiku poets are creating "a whole variety of poetics and criticisms, coexisting rather than competing."

That variety can be experienced in the following pages.

Cor van den Heuvel
New York City
Spring 1986

[7] *Haiku*, Vol. I, pp. 270, 272.

[8] *Frogpond*, VI, 4 (1983).

BOOK LIST (see Appendix C for information on books by the poets)

Amann, Eric W. *The Wordless Poem.* Haiku Magazine, Toronto, 1969.

Blyth, R. H. *Haiku.* Hokuseido Press, Tokyo, 1949–52. 4 vols.

———. *A History of Haiku.* Hokuseido Press, Tokyo, 1963–64. 2 vols.

———. *Japanese Life and Character in Senryu.* Hokuseido Press, Tokyo, 1960.

Brower, Gary. *Haiku in Western Languages.* Scarecrow Press, Metuchen, NJ, 1972.

Hackett, J. W. *The Zen Haiku and Other Zen Poems of J. W. Hackett.* Japan Publications, Tokyo, 1983 (distributed in the United States by Kodansha International through Harper & Row Publishers, 10 East 53rd Street, New York, NY 10022).

Henderson, Harold G. *The Bamboo Broom.* Houghton Mifflin, Boston, 1934.

———. *Haiku in English.* Japan Society, New York, 1965 (reprinted by Charles E. Tuttle Co., Rutland, VT, and Tokyo, 1967).

———. *An Introduction to Haiku.* Doubleday & Company, Garden City, NY, 1958.

Higginson, William J. *The Haiku Handbook: How to Write, Share, and Teach Haiku.* McGraw-Hill, New York, 1985.

Howard, Dorothy, and André Duhaime (eds. and trans.). *Haïku: Anthologie canadienne/Canadian Anthology.* Editions Asticou, Hull, Quebec, 1985.

Ichikawa Sanki (ed.). *Haikai and Haiku.* Nippon Gakujutsu Shinkokai, Tokyo, 1958.

Keene, Donald. *World Within Walls: Japanese Literature of the Pre-Modern Era, 1600–1867.* Holt, Rinehart and Winston, New York, 1976.

Miner, Earl. *Japanese Linked Poetry: An Account with Translations of Renga and Haikai Sequences.* Princeton University Press, Princeton, NJ, 1979.

——— and Hiroko Odagiri (trans.). *The Monkey's Straw Raincoat and Other Poetry of the Bashō School.* Princeton University Press, Princeton, NJ, 1981.

Sato, Hiroaki. *One Hundred Frogs: From Renga to Haiku to English.* Weatherhill, New York, 1983.

——— and Burton Watson (eds. and trans.). *From the Country of Eight Islands: An Anthology of Japanese Poetry.* Doubleday/Anchor, Garden City, NY, 1981.

Swede, George (ed.). *Canadian Haiku Anthology.* Three Trees Press, Toronto, 1979.

Ueda, Makoto. *Literary and Art Theories in Japan.* The Press of Case Western Reserve University, Cleveland, 1967.

———. *Matsuo Bashō.* Twayne Publishers, New York, 1970. A paperback edition has been published by Kodansha.

——— (ed. and trans.). *Modern Japanese Haiku: An Anthology.* University of Toronto Press, Toronto, 1976.

Willmot, Rod (ed.). *Erotic Haiku.* Black Moss Press, Windsor, Ontario, 1983.

Yasuda, Kenneth. *The Japanese Haiku.* Charles E. Tuttle Co., Rutland, VT, and Tokyo, 1957.

––––. *A Pepper Pod*. Alfred A. Knopf, New York, 1947. Reprinted as *A Pepper-Pod: A Haiku Sampler*, Charles E. Tuttle Co., Rutland, VT, and Tokyo, 1976.

MAGAZINES AND HAIKU PRESSES

Brussels Sprout, Alexis Rotella, editor, Box 72, Mountain Lakes, NJ 07046.

Burnt Lake Press, Rod Willmot, editor and publisher, 535 rue Duvernay, Sherbrooke, Quebec, J1L 1Y8.

Dragonfly, Richard Tice and Jack Lyon, editors, 7372 Zana Lane, Magna, UT 84044. Also publishes haiku chapbooks. Edited from 1973 to 1984 by Lorraine Ellis Harr.

Frogpond, Elizabeth Searle Lamb, editor, 970 Acequia Madre, Sante Fe, NM 87501. Magazine of the Haiku Society of America.

From Here Press, William J. Higginson, editor and publisher, Box 219, Fanwood, NJ 07023.

High/Coo Press, Randy and Shirley Brooks, editors and publishers, Route 1, Battle Ground, IN 47920. Publishes the *Haiku Review*, a biennial directory recording English language publications of the previous two years. Issued in '80, '82, '84 and continuing. Also publishes many small chapbooks of haiku and recently started a haiku magazine called *Mayfly*.

Inkstone, P.O. Box 67, Station "H," Toronto, M4C 5H7.

Modern Haiku, Robert Spiess, editor, P.O. Box 1752, Madison, WI 53701. Also publishes chapbooks.

Wind Chimes, Hal Roth, editor, P.O. Box 601, Glen Burnie, MD 21061. Also publishes chapbooks.

ORGANIZATIONS

Haiku Canada, 67 Court Street, Aylmer, Quebec, J9H 4M1.

Haiku Society of America, c/o Japan Society, 333 East 47th Street, New York, NY 10017.

Note: When writing to magazines, presses, or organizations enclose a stamped self-addressed envelope; if writing to one in another country, enclose an international reply coupon, which are available at the post office.

INTRODUCTION TO THE FIRST EDITION

Until now, the poets represented in this anthology have been largely "invisible." Though some of them have been writing haiku for nearly two decades or longer, their work has flowered practically unnoticed—their only recognition coming from the small world of the haiku magazines. The movement of which they are a part, however, has now reached a point where its accomplishments can no longer be ignored.

Haiku in English got its real start in the fifties, when an avid interest in Japanese culture and religion swept the post-war United States.[1] Growing out of the increased contacts with Japan through the Occupation and a spiritual thirst for religious and artistic fulfillment, this interest centered on art, literature, and Zen Buddhism. Alan Watts, Donald Keene, D. T. Suzuki, the Beats, and others all contributed to both arousing and feeding this interest, but it was R. H. Blyth's extraordinary four-volume work *Haiku* (published between 1949 and 1952), Kenneth Yasuda's *The Japanese Haiku* (1957), and Harold G. Henderson's *An Introduction to Haiku* (1958) that provided for the first time the solid foundation necessary for the creation of haiku in English.[2]

In the late fifties and early sixties the seed began to germinate, and a few poets across the country began to write haiku with an awareness and understanding of its possibilities.

---

[1] The Imagists, and those who followed them, had no real understanding of haiku. Because they had no adequate translations or critical analyses available, they failed to see the spiritual depth haiku embodies, or the unity of man and nature it reveals. English language haiku owes practically nothing to their experiments except in the sense that all modern poetry owes them a debt for their call for concision and clarity in language.

[2] Henderson published a small book on Japanese haiku, *The Bamboo Broom,* in 1934, in which he recognized the possibility of English haiku. But the time was not ripe. (There were exceptions: Clement Hoyt began studying Zen in 1936 with Nyogen Senzaki, the man who "taught me the haiku," and Yasuda was writing haiku in English in the thirties, publishing some as "Experiments in English" in *A Pepper Pod,* 1947.)

Within five years after the publication of Henderson's book, a magazine was started by James Bull in Platteville, Wisconsin, devoted solely to English language haiku: *American Haiku* (1963). The first issue was dedicated to Henderson and included a letter from him to the editors, which said in part: "If there is to be a real 'American Haiku' we must—by trial and error—work out our own standards. . . . One of the great functions *American Haiku* could perform is that of being a forum for the expression of divergent opinions." J. W. Hackett, Nicholas Virgilio, Mabelsson Norway (O Southard), and Larry Gates were among the contributors to that first issue.[3] The magazine was published twelve times in the next five years, ceasing publication in May 1968. Later that year, under the auspices of the Japan Society, the Haiku Society of America was founded to promote the writing and appreciation of haiku.

In the meantime, three new haiku magazines had emerged, all of which are still publishing. Jean Calkins started *Haiku Highlights and Other Small Poems* (now called *Dragonfly: A Quarterly of Haiku Highlights*) in Kanona, New York, in 1965. Though the work it published was undistinguished for a long time, in recent years it has printed significant articles on haiku by William J. Higginson, Michael McClintock, and others. In 1967 two haiku magazines appeared that were to carry on the work begun by *American Haiku: Haiku West,* edited by Leroy Kanterman in New York City, and *Haiku,* edited by Eric Amann in Toronto, Canada. (*Haiku* is now edited by William J. Higginson in Paterson, New Jersey.) Both have printed high-quality haiku, and *Haiku* has especially demonstrated a willingness to experiment with haiku form and presentation.

There are now at least five English language haiku magazines being published in the United States, with others in England and Australia. In fact, haiku are being written all over

[3] Among those appearing in the second issue were Robert Spiess, Virginia Brady Young, Clement Hoyt, and Elizabeth Searle Lamb.

the world—in German, French, Spanish, Portuguese, Italian, and other languages, as well as English and, of course, Japanese.[4]

In the midst of this proliferating interest and activity with haiku throughout the world, the "literary world"—critics and poets alike—continues to see English language haiku either as worthless fragments, blank and incomprehensible, or as little more than examples of a form of light verse whose only use is as an educational aid to interest children in poetry.[5] Such attitudes may have been excused in the early years—thousands of bad poems were published under the name of haiku—but in the last few years the proportion of good haiku to bad has been at least the same as in any other kind of poetry.

One can only conclude that such critics have not looked deeply enough into the literature available on the Japanese haiku and its esthetic traditions—or simply do not know haiku in English. Haiku is a poetry of simplicity and suggestion new to Western literature. It has been called "the wordless poem,"[6] and is often so bare as to seem meaningless to the uninitiated. Yet its few words have such an ontological immediacy that the sensitive reader can almost reach out and touch the things they

[4] See Gary Brower's annotated bibliography, *Haiku in Western Languages* (1972).

[5] There are exceptions. A few well-known poets have tried to write haiku, but none has seen it as a principal "way" or direction for their work. Gary Snyder, though he was one of the first to try writing haiku in English with an understanding of Japanese haiku (as early as 1952), has never concentrated his poetic energies in that direction. Jack Kerouac, the Beat novelist, was also an early practitioner of haiku, and probably came closer than any of the Beat poets to its essence. But it remained a footnote to his other work. More recently, Hayden Carruth, Robert Kelly, John Hollander, and some other recognized poets have experimented with short poems which derive from the form of haiku, but show little or no conception of the haiku's true nature.

[6] By Alan Watts. Eric Amann wrote an exceptionally fine book on haiku using this phrase for the title. It appeared as a special issue of *Haiku* in 1969.

describe. However commonplace the image, it is *now* in one of those timeless moments when it flashes forth an unspoken message of the oneness of existence. It does so in the silence that surrounds the words. Blyth has called haiku "an open door which looks shut," because it takes an intuitive awareness to see that moment of perception which lies just over the threshold. The reader must be an equal partner in the creative process—the slightest shift of focus or mood can close the door again. Aware readers are increasing, however, and the "visibility" of haiku in English will depend on their perception.

Haiku in English is still in the process of finding its "way." Beyond a general agreement that haiku should be short, concise, and immediate (or brief, simple, and direct, etc.), individual poets may often diverge widely in their conceptions of what a haiku is and how one is created. One of the most fundamental questions raised about haiku has been: is it basically a religious or an esthetic experience?

A number of those who favor the religious, or as some prefer to say, spiritual, side of this question relate haiku to the philosophy of Zen. J. W. Hackett and Eric Amann have been spokesmen for this view, which follows the "teachings" of R. H. Blyth. Citing Bashō—"Haiku is simply what is happening in this place, at this moment"—Hackett emphasizes haiku as a "way" of life, rather than as literature. In his book, *The Way of Haiku* (1969),[7] the poet states:

> I have written in the conviction that the best
> haiku are created from direct and immediate
> experience with nature, and that this intuitive
> experience can be expressed in any language.

[7] One of the very few haiku poets with a book readily obtainable at bookstores, Hackett alone has had a large body of work available for several years. A number of the poets in this anthology have, however, been published by small presses (see Appendix C: Biographies). [In 1983 Hackett published *The Zen Haiku and Other Zen Poems of J. W. Hackett*, which is a revised and enlarged edition of *The Way of Haiku*. It too contains the passage quoted above.]

> In essence I regard haiku as fundamentally ex-
> istential and experiential, rather than literary.
> There are, of course, important structural and
> artistic considerations involved in the expres-
> sion of the haiku experience . . .

In *Haiku in English* (1965), Henderson contrasts Hackett's approach ("what may loosely be called the Bashō school") with that of Nicholas Virgilio and others who stress imaginative creation—that is, the artistic role of the poet as a maker of imagined scenes as well as experienced ones, exemplified in Japanese haiku by Buson. Some poets who lean toward this view may believe their work is ultimately based on actual experience too, in the sense that even their imagined scenes are put together from things they have known. And since it is possible for *readers* to experience a "haiku moment" through words, even though they may never have encountered it in reality, there are poets who claim they can *discover* such moments in words during the creative process.

There is also the question of "natural speech" (artless) as opposed to language which uses poetic techniques. An argument against a too "literary" approach is R. H. Blyth's admonition that a bejewelled finger distracts from what it is pointing at. But it is well to keep in mind that a deformed finger can be distracting too, and may even point the wrong way.

The distinction between haiku and senryu, which are structurally similar, has also been a subject of controversy. Haiku is said to relate human nature to nature in general, while senryu is concerned primarily with human nature and is often humorous; but it is hard to draw the line.[8]

There are other differences among the haiku poets: there are the 5–7–5ers who believe haiku should be written in three lines of 5–7–5 syllables; then there are those who think the norm for English should be less than seventeen syllables to

---

[8] I have not tried to separate the senryu from the haiku in this book.

more closely approximate the actual length of seventeen Japanese *onji* (sound-symbols),[9] which are generally shorter than English syllables. Still others, like Michael McClintock, are for a "liberated haiku"—rejecting syllable-counting completely. There is the problem of subjectivity in haiku: is it allowable at all, and if so to what degree? And, on the other hand, is complete objectivity really possible?—and so on.

These "disputes" among the poets don't prevent them from appreciating each other's work, and are actually a way of answering Henderson's call to "work out our own standards." "Haiku" may be on its way to becoming a much broader term than it has been in the past. This may or may not be a good thing; but while some are working to broaden the concept, there are others who are moving toward a simpler, purer, deeper kind of haiku—and even a few who are finding ways to create poems which do both at once. Japanese haiku has survived countless controversies in its centuries-old history and haiku in English will too. As Henderson says, what haiku in English will become "will depend primarily on the poets who write them."[10]

A great diversity lies in the pages ahead. But though these poets are all moving along individual paths, they are all following the haiku "way." The variety of their voices should delight us as much as the oneness they reveal enlightens us. For the joy of life is to be able to see it anew each moment. These haiku moments await only your contribution of awareness.

Here you'll find the strange landscapes of Nicholas Virgilio, which, while remaining part of the real world, take us on a surrealistic trip to the source of the life force in a lily or to the mystery of death in the headlights of a funeral procession; or the simple wonders of J. W. Hackett, where a

[9] See Appendix B for definitions of "haiku" and related terms.

[10] *Haiku in English.*

caterpillar or a small cloud of gnats can take us to the core of existence simply by being what they are *now;* the daring experimentation of William J. Higginson or Anita Virgil, who both find new visceral possibilities in words; the muse-guided nature sensitivity of Mabelsson Norway, whose word-spells can call trees and rocks out of a timeless mist; the pure simplicity of Robert Spiess, the subtle clarity of whose images resonates again and again through the natural juxtaposition of the barest aspects of nature; the rich, fertile earth and living waters of John Wills; the haunting silences of Foster Jewell; the fresh virtuosity, sensual vigor, and delicacy of perception of Michael McClintock; and many more, all with their own individual voices, their own way of looking at the world through haiku.

There are undoubtedly poets and haiku missing from the following pages that belong here, but here at least is a representative selection—here is haiku in English becoming visible.

New York City
June 1973

THE
HAIKU
ANTHOLOGY

HELEN C. ACTON

Beads of spring rain
slipping slowly
down the wind chimes.

ERIC AMANN

The names of the dead
sinking deeper and deeper
into the red leaves

Quietly dozing
under a clock without hands:
the museum keeper

A night train passes:
pictures of the dead are trembling
on the mantelpiece

Winter burial:
a stone angel points his hand
at the empty sky

Billboards
wet
in spring
rain . . .

The circus tent
all folded up:
October mist . . .

Snow falling
on the empty parking-lot:
Christmas Eve . . .

NICK AVIS

freshly fallen snow—
opening a new package
of typing paper

the evening star
just above the snow the tip
of an alder bush

BOB BOLDMAN

Sitting
I follow my breath
out to where
the wind
meets the hazel pine

day darkens   in the shell

a fin
grazing on restless stars

I read
the feather
fallen on the page

walking with the river
     the water does my thinking

i end in shadow

a moment in the box of jade

in the heat
admiring the shade in the blouse

in the doll's
head
news clippings

mist,
panties on the line

face wrapping a champagne glass

JANUARY FIRST
the fingers of the prostitute cold

leaves blowing into a sentence

i hammer a nail
in the rain

touching the ashes of my father

just past sunset
frozen leaves stick
to the billboard

the priest
his shadow caught
on a nail

in the temple
a
heartbeat

JANICE BOSTOK

pregnant again . . .
the fluttering of moths
against the window

foetus kicks
the sky to the east
brilliant

CHUCK BRICKLEY

a few flakes appear
in the old prospector's pan—
winter morning sun

sheet lightning:
the face near the top
of the ferris wheel

the puppet
leaning from his booth
blinks at the rain

outside the pub
the sailor
faces the wind

deserted wharf
the mime bows
to the moon

autumn rain—
a dog looks up at each person
passing on the street

slipping in the snow
a child just lies there
eating it

spring evening—
playing with the last kitten
to be given away

summer evening—
the grandchild waves once more
at the empty road

MARTIN BURKE

rainy winter evening—
an inflatable doll sags
in the porno-shop window

on the twelfth floor
a life's work holds open
the book-reviewer's door

JACK CAIN

an empty elevator
opens
closes

waiting:
dry snowflakes fall
against the headlights

someone's newspaper
drifts with the snow
at 4 a.m.

empty room:
one swinging coat hanger
measures the silence

GERARD JOHN CONFORTI

On the mountain slope
the stillness of white pines
in the falling snow

RICHARD CRIST

the dusty pickup
turns into the farm lane—
kitchen lights go on

she has gone—
a vase of wild asters
on the kitchen table

L. A. DAVIDSON

in the dark lobby
of the residential hotel
a feeling of autumn

on my return
she brings blue plums
on a white plate

the silent crowd
waiting for the fountain
to rise again

it is growing dark,
no one has come to the door,
and still the dog barks

beyond
stars beyond
star

BETTY DREVNIOK

Deep snow:
peeling potatoes—
dark earth on my hands

Snow at dusk:
our pot of tea
steeps   slowly   darker

MICHAEL DUDLEY

menstrual cramps . . .
into the sink
she pours her coffee turned cold

at the backyard fence
my wife still laughing
with the widower

home late:
the cat's fur in patches
on her housecoat

lulling me to sleep
the rain
then waking me

LARRY GATES

The crow flies off . . .
   mountains fall away
    beneath him

Rowing
   out of the mist
      into the bright colors

On the jewelweed
   sparkling raindrops are falling
      from blossom to blossom

At the river-bend
   wriggling towards the setting sun
      a lone watersnake

The killdeer
  unmoved
    as the surf passes his feet

Winter dawn;
  from the deepest part of the forest
    crows are calling

The lights are going out
  in the museum, a fetus
    suddenly darkens

The silent Buddha
holding in his lap
a handful of shadows

LEROY GORMAN

beyond the laughing billboard girl
a hangglider
in the sun

her long paper legs
    smell
    of the river

down the billboard girl's bare belly
shadow
of a hawk

one AM
& the billboard girl's still up
with her lite on

billboard girl
only shadflies
have come to your lite

I shut down the lawnmower
a call for supper
over the still grass

my family asleep
I worry about money & count
fireflies in our garden

I hear her sew
I hear the rain
I turn back a page

loud wind
ashtray smoke curls
around the lamp

for the smell
I plane another shaving
snow buries my tracks from the house

ROSAMOND HAAS

Rain mixed with sleet:
in the small enclosed garden
the stone lantern darkens.

Building the dollhouse—
a monarch fans its wings
on a cross-beam

Autumn evening
   between thinning aspen leaves
      Orion's belt stars

Moon at the window:
water colors pooling
in an old egg carton

J. W. HACKETT

The stillness of dawn:
    crashing between the branches,
        a solitary leaf.

An old spider web
    low above the forest floor,
        sagging full of seeds.

Wind sounds through the trees . . .
    while here, gnats play in the calm
        of wooded sunlight.

Deep within the stream
the huge fish lie motionless
facing the current.

A bitter morning:
  sparrows sitting together
  without any necks.

Searching on the wind,
   the hawk's cry . . .
      is the shape of its beak.

Time after time
   caterpillar climbs this broken stem,
      then probes beyond.

Wind gives way to calm
   and the stream smoothes, revealing
      its treasure of leaves.

Moon fades into dawn . . .
an ivory moth settles
within the lily.

A long line of web
loose at both ends, riding free
on the summer breeze.

Half of the minnows
within this sunlit shallow
are not really there.

The fleeing sandpipers
turn about suddenly
and chase back the sea!

JIM HANDLIN

a full autumn moon
beneath white sealing wax
blackberry preserve

cold winter morning—
a chickadee chirps inside
the gargoyle's mouth

sunset—
the glass apple turns
red

LORRAINE ELLIS HARR

Indian summer:
   the scarecrow's jacket fades
     to a paler blue.

A pale dawn moon—
   furrows of the new-ploughed fields
     white with frost.

The time it takes—
   for snowflakes to whiten
     the distant pines.

After the snowfall . . .
deep in the pine forest
the sound of an axe.

Late snowfall;
   more and more yellow
      the forsythia.

Until it alights
   on a white daisy—just another
      blue dragonfly.

A hot summer wind—
   shadows of the windmill blades
      flow over the grass.

The sparkler goes out
   and with it—the face
      of the child.

On the old scarecrow
a crow sits for a while—
suddenly flies off.

PENNY HARTER

broken bowl
the pieces
still rocking

wrinkles
in the white icing
of the birthday cake

grandmother's mirror—
age spots
the glass

bitter tea—
in the empty cup
the folded lemon

in the mirror
the open door
blows shut behind me

winter rain
in our garage
the same stray cat

on the padlock
snow
melting

thawing
the dead field mouse
opens his mouth

snowflakes—
dust on the toes
of my boots

white flowers
in the snow

only letting in the cat
until
the morning star

the cat's whiskers
brushing tinsel

pine needles
in the broken curve
of the ornament

clouds
blowing off the stars

WILLIAM J. HIGGINSON

a robin listens
   then flies off
      snow eddies

this spring rain
the thief too
curses his job

Holding the water,
   held by it—
      the dark mud.

More intricate
than all winter's designs,
this spring flake.

writing again
the tea water
boiled dry

summer moon—
the only white
in the afternoon sky

before the descent
musing then seeing
the sudden bluebird

I look up
from writing
to daylight.

sky-black gull
       skims
  the wave inland
against the cliff
       whitens

              high tide—
              every now and then
              driftwood
              rocks

          the ducks land
          and turn on the swells
          to face the wind

evening star
almost within
the moon's half-curve

GARY HOTHAM

distant thunder
the dog's toenails click
against the linoleum

night comes—
picking up your shoes
still warm

up late—
the furnace comes on
by itself

my wife still asleep—
snow piles up
on the steps

morning quiet
snow sticking to this side
of the telephone poles

fog.
sitting here
without the mountains

on the ceiling
a large leak stain—
autumn coolness

waiting room quiet
    an apple core
  in the ashtray

stalled car.
foot tracks being filled
with snow.

coffee
in a paper cup—
a long way from home

the library book
overdue—
slow falling snow

every night
the same shop—
the stuffed hawk's beak shines

home early—
your empty coat hanger
in the closet

this loneliness
the rain continues
into darkness

letting
the dog out—
the stars out

morning fog
not seeing far
the fern's underside

unsnapping
the holster strap
summer heat

sunset dying
on the end of a rusty
beer can . . .

quietly
the fireworks
far away

sun & moon
in the same sky
the small hand of my wife

CLEMENT HOYT

While the guests order,
the table cloth hides his hands—
counting his money.

Down from the bridge rail,
   floating from under the bridge,
      strangers exchange stares.

The pretty matron,
   sure she is pregnant again,
      smashes potted plants.

Those camellias,
   grown by the town embalmer,
      won the prize again.

In that empty house,
   with broken windows rattling,
     a door slams and slams.

Leaves moil in the yard,
   reveal an eyeless doll's head . . .
     slowly conceal it.

In that lightning flash—
   through the night rain—I saw it!
     . . . whatever it was.

A Hallowe'en mask,
   floating face up in the ditch,
     slowly shakes its head.

Hair, in my comb's teeth,
   the color of autumn wind—
      this whole day is gray.

Last screech owl cry—
How quietly the dawnlight
comes creeping through the woods.

Thunder storm passing—
echoing along the shore
that last hollow sound . . .

This evening stillness . . .
just the rusted cowbell
found by the pasture gate.

That breeze brought it—
a moment of moonlight
to the hidden fern.

Nearing the mountain
yesterday, and still today . . .
tomorrow.

Disturbing some brush,
and after miles and miles . . .
still the rattling sound.

Cliff dweller ruins
and the silence of swallows
encircling silence.

Somewhere behind me,
seeming in dark-silence
to feel a slow coiling.

Some unknown sound . . .
the looking behind me—
the looking all around.

Where the coyote called,
rising in full cry, the moon . . .
the sound of silence.

Fall wind in pinyons . . .
Faster and louder patters
   yesterday's shower.

Mountain shadow
crossing the evening river
at the old fording place.

Under ledges
and looking for the coolness
that keeps touching my face.

Finding this cavern—
following the lantern light . . .
followed by silence.

JACK KEROUAC

In my medicine cabinet,
  the winter fly
has died of old age.

Birds singing
  in the dark
—Rainy dawn.

Straining at the padlock,
  the garage doors
At noon

Arms folded
  to the moon,
Among the cows.

Missing a kick
  at the icebox door
It closed anyway.

GUSTAVE KEYSER

In the wake
of a gliding swan
ducks rocking

Rainy summer night . . .
shadow of a quiet moth
inside the lamp shade

TADASHI KONDO

autumn light
the puppeteer
eating alone

ELIZABETH SEARLE LAMB

broken kite, sprawled
on a sand dune, its line caught
in the beach plum . . .

the far shore
drifting out of the mist
to meet us

a lizard inching
with the shadow of the stone
nearer the cave's mouth

far back under a ledge
the ancient petroglyph   faintly
water sound

still . . . some echo
the pale jade cricket box
in the museum

pausing
halfway up the stair—
white chrysanthemums

shimmering beneath the glaze,
blue brush strokes
on the Chinese ginger jar

the old album:
not recognizing at first
my own young face

leaving   all the morning glories   closed

RUTH LATTA

A hand reaches up
and pulls down
a shade.

DAVID E. LECOUNT

The bridge toll-booth—
from the dark a hand collects
rain on the coins.

GERALDINE CLINTON LITTLE

Fallen horse—
flies hovering
in the vulture's shadow

The white spider
  whiter still
    in the lightning's flash

now ice-covered
  trapping a hundred moons—
    paperwasp's hive

DAVID LLOYD

Quietly shaping
The hollow of the blossom
The morning sunrise

Wild rose bending—
And bending even more
With the bee's weight

Over dried grass,
Two butterflies—
And a chill wind . . .

Duck feathers
On the lake's shore—
Silent skies

Moonlit sleet
In the holes of my
Harmonica

At the bottom
Of the rocky mountain slope,
A pile of pebbles

The longest night:
Only the snowman stares
At the stars

PEGGY LYLES

Summer stillness
the play of light and shadow
on the windchimes

A doe's leap
darkens the oyster shell road:
twilight

Moon
and melon cooling
with us in the stream

Summer night:
we turn out all the lights
to hear the rain

MATSUO ALLARD

an icicle the moon drifting through it

snow by the window paper flowers gathering dust

thawing ice the garbage blooming out of it

the silence a droplet of water trickles down a stone

passing clouds only a stand of aspens is in light

alone tonight one fish ripples the lake

deep in my notebook a lily pad floats away

MICHAEL MCCLINTOCK

overtaken
by a single cloud,
and letting it pass . . .

the bluebird alights
     at once
on the bright wet twig

long summer day . . .
     my neighbor's bull
        at it again

   peering out
the scarecrow's ear—
   two glittering eyes

a grasshopper
jumped into it:
summer dusk

a small girl . . .
the shadows stroke
and stroke her

the merry-go-round
as it turns
shines into the trees

look it's clear
to Saturn

glimmering morning
silence unfolds all
the yucca

across the sands
the rippling quiet
cloud shadow

a side-canyon:
pausing a moment, listening
into its reach . . .

rowing downstream
red leaves   swirling
behind me

i eat alone
& pass the salt
for myself

letting my tongue
    deeper into the cool
        ripe tomato

a broken window
    reflects half the moon,
        half of me

hearing
  cockroach feet;
    the midnight snowfall

Hamburger Hill . . .
the full moon
in our eyes

a drizzling rain . . .
washing their blood
into their blood

tonight . . . wishing
the lightning were lightning
the thunder, thunder

dead cat . . .
open-mouthed
to the pouring rain

thought i'd
never grow old
today met a kid
said to me
"Mister"

hungry
without money—
after awhile
stopt pretending
ate a parsnip

sat down
to enjoy the view
the beauty of it
suddenly
gone

here's a guy
sits on his mat
like Buddha
but here's one
that just sits

pushing
   inside . . . until
      her teeth shine

the first melt . . .
   her eyes gone
      under their lids

while we wait
to do it again,
the rains of spring

she leaves—
   warm pillow scent
     remaining

twisting inland,
the sea fog takes awhile
in the apple trees

a single tulip!
hopelessly,
i passed on

a poppy . . .
a field of poppies!
the hills blowing with poppies!

evening lecture
a shadow hangs
from the pointing finger

her silence at dinner
sediment
            hanging in the wine

crying
she moves deeper
into the mirror

with the last lamp
stripping
her shadow off

moonrise   white cat eating the cardinal

LENARD D. MOORE

Summer noon;
the blueberry field divided
by a muddy road

farther and farther
into the mountain trail
autumn dusk deepens

stars
flickering . . .
snow

silent deer   the sound of a waterfall

MARLENE MOUNTAIN

end of the cold spell
i'd forgotten the color
of my under socks

wood pile
on the sagging porch
unstacking itself

pig and i spring rain

empty mailbox
i pick wildflowers
on my way back

he leans on the gate going staying

a quiet day
an old man on his tractor
passes at dusk

on this cold
        spring   1
    2 night 3   4
        kittens
        wet
        5

at dusk hot water from the hose

            pick-up truck
        guns on the window rack
            the heat

                                        one fly everywhere the heat

        summer night clothes whirling in a dryer

f

r

o

g

f   frog

gosling following its neck to the bug

my neighbor's rooster hops the   stick   i throw

old towel   folding it again   autumn evening

in
the
woods a
sudden
backlit
leaf

in her old voice the mountains

beneath
leaf mold
stone
cool
stone

faded flowers of the bed sheets autumn night

after your visit
middle of the closet
empty hangers

smoke from a neighbor's chimney   loneliness

seed catalog in the mailbox   cold drizzle

```
        k k k k k
      c c c c c c c
      o o o o o o o
      c c c c c c c
        a a a a a
          e e e
            p
```

```
              O
            O
      c o y O t e
```

```
          rain
        dr  p
          o
```

krïk′ït

hoot
w
l

sn wfl k s

ALAN PIZZARELLI

driving
out of the car wash

clouds move
across the hood

    bending back
along the railroad track
                tiger lilies

a bright awning is cranked
over the corner fruitstand

just before dawn
a beachball   floats
across the stillness of the pool

lightens

flinging the frisbee
skips off the ground
    curving up   hits a tree

    petals

a piece of buttered popcorn
floats in the garden pond
    swirling colors

       buzzZ
              slaP
       buzzZ

waterbug running by the frogulp

              scarecrow
              coughs
              butterflies

the fat lady
bends over the tomatoes
a full moon

the bearded lady
hangs her wash
against the wind

the tattoo'd man
walks onto the crowded beach

the brim-shadow
of the fat man's straw hat
lowers over a long sandwich

late in the evening
a midget hoses the sunflowers

drop of ocean
in my navel
reflects
the Amusement Park

under the boardwalk
bullet shells glint
below the shooting gallery

on the merry-go-round
that empty blue bench

PORNO MOVIE

      the girl
         loosens her bra
   starts peeling off panties
        darkens

    25¢

opening the mailbox
nothing but a screak

a stranger passing
    starts saying something
his hat falls off

    Fwap!
colored balls scatter
in the green poolhall

a spark
falls to the ground
            darkens

that's it

tonite
nothing to write

but this

tiny fish
swaying
into the current
shadows rippling
over a hubcap

Just before the storm
a deflated basketball
falls into its shadow

                    a moving van zooms
along the backroads

                    autumn

meteor

the cloud fades back
into blackness

snow falls from trees
rumble
of passing boxcars

the shade springs open
frozen socks on the line

with no money
I go
snow viewing

sun brightens
snow   slides off
the car bumper

wiping the chrome
blue vapors fade

CLAIRE PRATT

The fog has settled
around us. A faint redness
where the maple was.

MARJORY BATES PRATT

Not a breath of air—
   only a water bug mars
   the pine's reflection.

FRANK K. ROBINSON

the down rippling
on a gray moth's back—
cold autumn wind

today too
snow on my mailbox
undisturbed

brief day ending
    the angel's stone wings
tipped with fire

EMILY ROMANO

August heat;
the coolness of eggs
in a blue crock

the banker
cancels
a moth

flea . .
that you,
Issa?

after *Tosca*
a mosquito
aria

the sailor
peeling potatoes
around himself

pacing
the shore
the ship's cat

brushing my sins
the muscatel breath
of the priest

the cat
lowers his ears
to the master's fart

after Beethoven
he gets the furnace
roaring

white orchid
on her coffin
　　　the pickle lady

rain
erasing
the clown's face

on the apple
the white butterfly
is pink

the black hen
eating outside
her shadow

the blind man's
yellow pencil
in the rain

ordering my tombstone
the cutter has me feel
his Gothic "R"

Sistine Chapel:
just above me the snug arc
of a toenail

under
El Greco
the brown bag lunch

blues are the big thing
with Monet, she said,
spreading the Roquefort

unable
        to get hibiscus red
the artist eats the flower

     piano practice
through an open window
       the lilac

buttoning his fly
the boy with honeysuckle
clenched in his mouth

     in white tulips
the rooster's red head
     flowering

birthcry!
　　　the stars
　　　are all in place

seance
a white
moth

campfire extinguished,
the woman washing dishes
in a pan of stars

he removes his glove
　　　to point out
　　　　　　　Orion

takes in
the world
from the heart out

funnels
our day
into itself

closes
on its own
inner light

SYDELL ROSENBERG

Library closing—
the sleeping wino wakes up
holding a shut book.

In the laundermat
  she peers into the machine
    as the sun goes down.

ALEXIS ROTELLA

At the edge
of the inkstone
butterfly fanning

From green to grey
a lizard crawls out
of the coloring book

A rainbow
escapes
the shattered crystal vase

From her neon window
the crystal gazer
stares into winter rain

in the Queen Anne's lace a toad

Undressed—
today's role dangles
from a metal hanger

asparagus   I bite off their heads

Trying to forget him
stabbing
the potatoes

surrendering to a rain-washed stone

starrynightIenteryourmirror

Leading him in . .
my bracelet
jangling

in his wedding band watching the clouds pass

Lying in the wet grass,
him still beating
inside me

swans   stir of his breath against my hair

With wine glasses
we stand and talk
into the rhododendrons

His footsteps in the room
above me: slowly
I brush my hair

Holding his gaze
the night's trees
stand still

Waterlilies . .
in a moment he'll ask me
what I'm thinking

Late August
I bring him the garden
in my skirt

Barefoot through clover
for a moment
I forget my yearning

Not speaking
our shadows
keep touching

After the full moon
shadows
under my eyes

Against his coat
I brush my lips—
the silence of snowflakes

In the garbage bin
mound of snow
and a valentine

Everyone talking at once
the galaxy
in my moonstone

Only I laugh
at his joke . .
the silence

Opening his
dresser drawer—
darkness slips out

From the window
watching him plant the garden
alone

During our argument
a pink rose
tightens its petals

Clutching a fist of hair
from my brush
I watch him sleep

Discussing divorce
he strokes
the lace tablecloth

After he leaves
I cry aloud
to the room

Phone call
his three-day stubble
scraping the distance

In the guest room
where my mother slept
I look for comfort

Left to the wind
all the lilies
and all his lies

Breakfast alone—
three bouquets of mums
drinking from the sink

Vase of peonies:
on a white bud
lipstick print

a butterfly lands on Park Place

HAL ROTH

evening star
in line with the lamp
in her window

argument ended
her pearl earring reflects
the candle flame

her black negligee
its left strap
off the hanger

her eyes still closed
white curtains
in morning sun

HIROAKI SATO

In your panties
slightly pulled down
a crisp fallen leaf

the silence
while the gift
is being opened

MICHAEL SEGERS

in the eggshell after the chick has hatched

MARTIN SHEA

warehouse-theatre's
muffled cries the
soft night rain

red-flashing lights
on the leaves by the window—
they draw down the shade

through the wall
　　crying . . . or
not crying

those corner winds—
the bible-thumper . . .
thumps

caught shoplifting—
crying, she beats her child
for wanting the toy

walk's end . . .
　　the cold of his hand
　　shook mine

bolted   space

the lights on the corners
click and change

held it,
a peony
        —black Rolls

Moving
    through the criteria—
            a breeze.

sparrows sunning
on the slaughterhouse

terminal.
one far off and
perfect moon

the long night
of the mannequins—
snow falling

O. MABSON SOUTHARD

Down to dark leaf-mold
the falling dogwood-petal
carries its moonlight

Now the leaves are still—
and only the mockingbird
lets the moonlight through!

In the garden pool,
dark and still, a stepping-stone
releases the moon

The old rooster crows...
Out of the mist come the rocks
and the twisted pine

On a leaf, a leaf
  casts a swaying green shadow—
    and the tree-frog sings!

Gleaming—sunken stones…
With her shadow, the catfish
turns them off and on

A patter of rain…
The lily-pad undulates
on widening rings

Perching bolt upright—
the crow lets the rain-water
trickle from her tail.

Across the still lake
through upcurls of morning mist—
the cry of a loon

Mirrored by the spring
    under the pines, a cluster
      of Indian-pipes

Hushed, the lake-shore's pines...
    Once more a steady mountain
      rests on steady clouds

Still sunlit, one tree...
    Into the mountain-shadow
      it lets fall a leaf

This morning's rainbow
  shares its deep violet edge
    with the misty moon

One breaker crashes...
  As the next draws up, a lull—
    and sandpiper-cries

The waves now fall short
  of the stranded jellyfish...
    In it shines the sky

In the sea, sunset...
On the dark dune, a bright fringe
of waving grasses

Steadily it snows...
    Under the shadowy pines—
      where are the shadows?

Snow-laden bushes—
    one bent to the ground, and one
      swaying in the wind

On the top fence-rail
    she lights, knocking off some snow—
      a common sparrow

At the window, sleet...
Here in the darkening hut—
sudden squeaks of mice

1
Overwhelmed by mist
the rocky peak struggles out—
and sinks back under

2
My snow down her neck
my sister laughs, and shudders,
and kisses my mouth

3
Staining the cliff dark
with afternoon meltwater—
a cornice of snow

4

Lodged in the plunge-pool
  the trunk of a broken tree
    parts the waterfall

5

Under the cool pines
  the path dips round a boulder
    and climbs to a ledge

6

By her childhood name
  I call and call my sister—
    and so do the cliffs

ROBERT SPIESS

Blue jays in the pines;
the northern river's ledges
cased with melting ice

Marsh marigold
  on a low island of grass;
    the warmth of the sun

Patches of snow
  mirrored in the flowing stream;
    a long wedge of geese

Tar paper cabin
  behind the river's white birch
    —a muskellunge leaps

Muttering thunder . . .
the bottom of the river
scattered with clams

A light river wind;
  on the crannied cliff
    hang harebell and fern

Shooting the rapids!
  —a glimpse of a meadow
    gold with buttercups

Lean-to of tin;
  a pintail on the river
    in the pelting rain

A dirt road . . .
   acres of potato plants
      white-flowered under the moon

Asparagus bed
   silent in the morning mist
      the wild turkeys

Dry, summer day;
   chalk-white plover mute
      on a mid-stream rock

Becoming dusk,—
the catfish on the stringer
swims up and down

Ostrich fern on shore;
a short-eared owl in an oak
watching the canoe

A long wedge of geese;
straw-gold needles of the larch
on the flowing stream

Wispy autumn clouds;
in the river shallows
the droppings of a deer

Winter wind—
    bit by bit the swallow's nest
    crumbles in the barn

The chain saw stops;
    deeper in the winter woods
    a chickadee calls

Winter moon;
a beaver lodge in the marsh,
mounded with snow

GEORGE SWEDE

Swinging on the hanger
her white summer dress:
wind chimes

Night begins to gather   between her breasts

On the face
that last night called me names—
morning sunbeam

Unhappy wife
I pedal my bike
through puddles

Panties on the clothesline   lingering mist

One buttton undone
in the clerk's blouse—I let her
steal my change

One by one to the floor   all of her shadows

Christmas Eve:
in the massage parlour window—
reduced rates

Leaving my loneliness   inside her

At dawn   remembering her bad grammar

At the end of myself   pencil tip

Mental hospital   my shadow stays outside

Dawn
the face in the mirror
never smiles

After the search for meaning   bills in the mail

In one corner
of the mental patient's eye
I exist

At the edge of the precipice   I become logical

Dawn
weathervane rooster
creaks

Passport check:
my shadow waits
across the border

in the town dump I find a still-beating heart

At my father's
distant grave—someone
has left flowers

Summer night:
in my eyes starlight
hundreds of years old

Windless summer day:
the gentle tug of the current
on the fishing pole

The August sky
jammed with stars   from the hilltop
I shine back

stars   crickets

After I step
through the moonbeam—
I do it again

The frozen breaths
of the carolers   disappearing
among the stars

A wisp of spring cloud
   drifting apart from the rest . . .
    slowly evaporates.

After gazing at stars . . .
   now, I adjust to the rocks
    under my sleeping bag.

The tinkle of chimes
   mingles with the steady fall
    of the autumn rain . . .

JAMES TIPTON

all day
    shoveling sheep manure
the mind clear at last

COR VAN DEN HEUVEL

a tidepool
in a clam shell
the evening sunlight

summer breeze
again the whirligig duck flaps
toward the sea

starting to rise
to the top of the wave
the cormorant dives into it

twilight
a breeze along the boardwalk
spins all the pinwheels

raining at every window

after the shower
listening to my
self drip

my mind takes a leap
off the baseboard
in the bathroom

hot night
turning the pillow
to the cool side

from behind me
the shadow of the ticket-taker
comes down the aisle

autumn twilight—
in the closed barbershop
the mirrors darken

a stick goes over the falls at sunset

November evening—
the wind from a passing truck
ripples a roadside puddle

a branch
waves in the window
and is gone

the shadow in the folded napkin

late autumn—
the great rock reappears
in the woods

the sun goes down
my shovel strikes a spark
from the dark earth

the geese have gone—
in the chilly twilight
empty milkweed pods

after posting the letter
staring at the slot—
winter rain

nothing
in the box—
the winter wind

in the hotel lobby
the bare bulb of a floor lamp
shines down on its distant base

tundra

shading his eyes
the wooden Indian looks out
at the spring rain

in the parking lot
a cloud drifts
from bumper to bumper

through the small holes
in the mailbox
sunlight on a blue stamp

ANITA VIRGIL

a phoebe's cry . . .
the blue shadows
on the dinner plates

twilight
taking
the trees

the black spaces:
as much star
as star!

Awakening . . .
the cold fresh scent:
new snow.

over & over
my silver needle catches
the morning sun

walking the snow-crust
not sinking
sinking

Darkening
the cat's eyes:
a small chirp.

morning bath
clouds & birds float between
still wet limbs

spring breeze . . .
her breasts sway
over the porcelain tub

she turns the child
to brush her hair
with the wind

holding you
in me still . . .
sparrow songs

the dark
throbbing
with spring
peepers

The first hot night:
chilling the tea,
slicing the lemons.

the coal train
slow along
summer foothills

low tide:
all the people
stoop

Another year!
the rugman comes to clean
the same rug . . .

A rainy day—
even the toiletpaper
comes to pieces!

bitterness
from an empty hearth
summer coolness

knifing deep
into earth seeking
the whole mushroom

red flipped out
chicken lung
in a cold white sink

Emerging hot and rosy
from their skins—
beets!

Laughing softly
under the trees
of the cemetery

behind sunglasses
I doze and wake . . .
the friendly man talks on

hot afternoon . . .
only the slap slap
of a jumprope

Claiming
the outhouse roof:
peacock!

not seeing
the room is white
until that red apple

the swan's head
turns away from sunset
to his dark side

Quiet afternoon:
water shadows
on the pine bark.

mullein
with nothing around it
but the air

trickling
over the dam—
summer's end

NICHOLAS VIRGILIO

Lily:
    out of the water . . .
    out of itself.

At the open grave
   mingling with the priest's prayer:
   honking of wild geese.

In the empty church
   at nightfall, a lone firefly
   deepens the silence.

Lone red-winged blackbird
riding a reed in high tide—
billowing clouds.

Heat before the storm:
　　a fly disturbs the quiet
　　　of the empty store.

The junkyard dog
　　in the shadow of the shack:
　　　the heat.

The empty highway:
　　a tiger swallowtail
　　　follows the divider.

The town clock's face
　adds another shade of yellow
　　to the afterglow.

A distant balloon
　drifting over the county fair,
　　eclipses the moon.

Town barberpole
　stops turning:
　　autumn nightfall.

Now the swing is still:
a suspended tire
centers the autumn moon.

The cathedral bell
   is shaking a few snowflakes
     from the morning air.

A crow in the snowy pine . . .
   inching up a branch,
     letting the evening sun through.

Winter evening
   leaving father's footprints:
     I sink into deep snow.

The sack of kittens
sinking in the icy creek,
increases the cold.

Deep in rank grass,
through a bullet-riddled helmet:
an unknown flower.

—In memory of Corporal
Lawrence J. Virgilio, USMC

The autumn wind
   has torn the telegram and more
     from mother's hand.

Flag-covered coffin:
   the shadow of the bugler
     slips into the grave.

My gold star mother
   and father hold each other
     and the folded flag.

Viet Nam Monument
   darkened by the autumn rain:
     my dead brother's name.

My dead brother . . .
  hearing his laugh
    in my laughter.

Another autumn
  still silent in his closet:
    father's violin.

My dead brother . . .
  wearing his gloves and boots:
    I step into deep snow.

The hinge of the year:
  holding up candles in church
    lighting up our breaths.

Pressing my forehead
  against my palsied mother's:
    sharing my ashes.

After father's wake
  the long walk in the moonlight
    to the darkened house.

Adding father's name
  to the family tombstone
    with room for my own.

Alone on the road
  in the wake of the hearse:
    dust on my shoes.

Into the blinding sun . . .
the funeral procession's
glaring headlights.

Beyond empty pews
darkened to a dying candle:
a bell tolls and tolls.

Autumn twilight:
the wreath on the door
lifts in the wind.

LARRY WIGGIN

scouring pans—
snow deepening
in the yard

dreaming . . .
dust
on the window

wind:
the long hairs
on my neck

fly
on the flank
of the bronze horse

crickets . . .
then
thunder

her breasts lift with her arms
flowers on the curtains
fold and unfold

I find her huddled on the bed
the paperback
closing by itself

If I go alone,
I'll lie in the wildflowers
　　　　and dream of you

A page of Shelley
brightens and dims
        with passing clouds

weak sun
silverware dries cold
under the open window

cheeses, pâté
my mouth suddenly dry
when she looks at him

humiliated again
bar-smoke in the sweater
I pull from my head

her hand on the doorknob—
   sunlight streams
     between her legs

away from eyes
the stairwell holds
us in its arms

shadows in the grass
our feet grow cool
as we talk of lost friends

now the spade
sinks by itself
fireflies turning the dark

A quiet rustle
    through the leaves . . .
stirring together in our sleep

mail on the counter
sits unopened
afternoon sun through birches

novel's end
on the cluttered desk
a pool of clear wood

musty shed
winter light
on the overturned canoe

Listening . . .
After a while,
I take up my axe again

JOHN WILLS

boulders
just beneath the boat
it's dawn

water pools
among the rocks   pools
and pools again

the river
leans upon the snag
a moment

a bluegill rises
to the match   wavers
and falls away

white horse
in the meadow
nosing clouds

larger
than the wren himself
the wren joy

laurel in bloom
she lingers awhile
at the mirror

goats on the roof
of the chicken shack
spring morning

my hand moves out
touches the sun
on a log

the old cow lags
to loll and splash
spring evening

the moon at dawn
lily pads blow white
in a sudden breeze

rain in gusts
below the deadhead
troutswirl

a bittern booms
in the silence that follows
smell of the marsh

summer drizzle
butterflies deep
in the grasses

a bluejay sails
to the bough of a pine
the coolness

below the dam
the great clouds
spreading out

the hills
release the summer clouds
one   by one   by one

a stagnant pond
red dragonflies
the heat

water lilies
slithering through them
a leech

beyond the porch
the summer night   leaning out
a moment

the sun lights up a distant ridge   another

a mourning cloak
comes sailing down
the deerpath

the forest stands
so straight and tall
at noon

looking deeper
and deeper into it
the great beech

coolness
hemlock shadows flicker
across the boulder

i catch
the maple leaf   then let
it go

the day wears on
the logcock keeps on
drumming

dusk   from rock to rock a waterthrush

den of the bear
beyond the great rocks
storm clouds

a pebble falls
bushes at the water's edge
just faintly glimmer

the evening sun
slips over the log   follows me
downriver

another bend
now at last   the moon
and all the stars

november evening
the faintest tick of snow
upon the cornstalks

in an upstairs room
of the abandoned house
a doll moongazing

winter again
my wife's hair crackles
under the comb

a box of nails
on the shelf of the shed
the cold

RUTH YARROW

sunrise path:
at each step the baby's shadow
releases her foot

the baby's pee
pulls roadside dust
into rolling beads

low winter moon:
her cheek curves the shadow
of the crib bar

warm rain before dawn:
my milk flows into her
unseen

KENNETH YASUDA

A crimson dragonfly,
As it lights, sways together
With a leaf of rye.

On the bench I wait
For the second gust to come
Through the garden gate.

A crimson dragonfly,
Glancing the water, casts rings
As it passes by.

The shadow of the trees
Almost reaches to my desk
With the summer breeze.

VIRGINIA BRADY YOUNG

On the first day of spring
snow falling
from one bough to another

In a circle of thaw
   the cat walks
      round and round

The sight of a lark's
throat throbbing! A woman
shelling peas . . .

Violets
in a broken sac of dew:
the hoof of a deer . . .

at twilight
hippo
    shedding
    the river

persimmons
lightly swaying—
    heavy with
    themselves

fallen birch leaf
  vein-side
    to the sky

The silence
in moonlight
of stones

ARIZONA ZIPPER

A farmer drives by,
  after a thundershower,
    with his manure cart.

The football
  hops off the field—
    with a toad.

The wedding over,
  he listens to her snore
    and lights another pipe.

Right in the middle
  of the cat's yawn—
    a pink tongue.

I stop to listen;
the cricket
has done the same.

APPENDIX A

I: Renga

Renga—also called "linked-verse poems" and "renku"—
can be written by one poet (solo renga) but are usually com-
posed by two or more poets writing verses, or links, in turn. In
Japan this is done during live sessions, but in the West renga
have most often been written through the mail. Japanese renga
alternate verses of 5-7-5 *onji* with verses of 7-7 *onji,* so most
Western renga have been written alternating 3-line links with
2-line links. A few have been written alternating short and
long 1-line links. The usual lengths of Japanese renga are 36
or 100 verses.

Each link should form a complete poem with the link that
immediately follows it, and another complete poem with the
one that comes before it. Often the meaning of a particular
link will change as it is considered first with the one preceding
it, and then with the one succeeding it. And of these three
there may be no relationship at all between the first and last.
The only link that must be able to stand alone is the hokku, the
"starting link" of the complete renga.

One common form of linking is narrative connection—
though any two links connected in this way usually have other

relationships linking them too. In fact, renga has been called narrative without plot, or broken narrative. Because of the changing relationships among the links, any one narrative "line" may go on for only two links (though it can go on for more) before it is replaced by a new one. A link might have no narrative, or any other, relationship with any link in the renga except those links immediately preceding and following it. *The Ragged Mists Renga,* however, retains a recurring narrative theme, or at least the impression of one, and a rough semblance of a plot may be reconstructed from it—though none was intended.

In addition to narrative connections, linking in renga is accomplished by various kinds of association or relationship, involving contrasts as well as similarities. Matsuo Bashō (1644–1694), Japan's greatest master of both renga and haiku, named at least five types of relationship: *nioi* (fragrance or scent), *hibiki* (echo or reverberation), *utsuri* (movement, change, or reflection), *kurai* (rank or degree), and *omokage* (allusion or mental image). Descriptions of renga techniques and methods of composition can be found in Maeda Cana's introduction to her translation of Bashō's *Monkey's Raincoat,* in Makoto Ueda's *Matsuo Bashō,* in Earl Miner's books on linked poetry, in Hiroaki Sato's *One Hundred Frogs,* and in William J. Higginson's *The Haiku Handbook.* The last two also contain renga by English language poets.

The sample renga in this section include one by three poets and one solo renga. *The Ragged Mists Renga* was written through the mail by three American haiku poets: John Wills in Tennessee, Cor van den Heuvel in New Jersey, and Michael McClintock in California. They took turns writing the links in the order in which their names are given. It was decided to end with the "hub-cap" link (by van den Heuvel), so McClintock wrote one fewer than the others. These are rather short renga; the usual length in the West has been thirty-six links, the length favored by Bashō.

The Ragged Mists Renga

BY JOHN WILLS, COR VAN DEN HEUVEL,
AND MICHAEL MCCLINTOCK

the winter mountains—
below, through ragged mists . . .
the leaves of spring

twenty TV screens glow
in the christmas tree ornament

the doll's house . . .
onto the crooked step
drops a pine needle

at 8 p.m. the Rolls stops
in front of her gate and honks

the light goes out
the boy next door backs away
from his own reflection

rereading this koan
pain of ankles crossed

wading the flats
of the limpid river . . .
the mountains beyond

a stick floats from the shadows
followed by a shadow

against the bathers'
white thighs
plash the autumn colors

in her dining room
the wallpaper is gaudy

beyond the doorway:
blood-spattered legs
in the glare of a flashbulb

incense . . . the ash tip
              falls off

here and there
the branch swirls darkly
above the snow

morning sunlight drifts down
from the wooded cliffs

piled on the beach
the crabs
grip one another

the grassy knoll beyond her thigh
rises, then subsides

licking the dripping lips—
through the open window,
the sound of skipping rope

click of a key;
cold corridor

even the tom
in the weeds outside
walks stiffly

my winter coat—
her scarf in the sleeve

blackness;
what the wind
blew onto the porch

the neighbor's milkcow
bawling in the mist

a hub cap
at the side of the road—
the sun comes and goes

BLAZING TIDEFLATS
A Solo Renga

BY COR VAN DEN HEUVEL

blazing tideflats—
the clam's
darkness

a dolphin leaps over
the wake of the boat

in the picture book
a pop-up figure of a cowboy
stands with a bent carbine

the christmas tree lights
in the toy dog's eye

on the windowsill
drifted snow marked
with bird tracks

walking around the deserted cabin
looking for a trail out

above the hills
the darkened sky grows darker—
wink of a plane

alone in the waiting room,
my body waits for my mind

a masked doctor
pushes an empty wheelchair
along the corridor

the scream breaks into sobs—
all the lights shine in her face

the men look
at each other and smile—
"print it!"

the pigeons all rise at once
and disappear around the corner

in front of the bank—
wondering where the money
went

dipping with every ripple
a popsicle-stick in the gutter stream

hesitating at the top,
the roller coaster hangs above the beach—
then thunders out of sight

the wave pulls back leaving
rolling pebbles in its wake

spring breeze for a thousand miles—
the wet tundra ripples and flutters
in the morning sunlight

the speckled eggs in the nest,
the speckled petals of the flower

standing up
from the blueberry bush—
the lake through the trees

wondering if anyone lives
in this forest wilderness

the sun goes out
on the raised paddle—
a chill wind comes off the mountain

"the Indians made offerings
to the spirit of the falls"

putting down the book
on Champlain's explorations
to look at the water in the glass

the candles glow softly—
blackout in New York City

moonlight—
a great liner, all lit up,
heads out to sea

II: Sequences

At least one critic has said that the following sequences by Marlene Mountain are free-verse poems and should not have been printed in the haiku magazines in which they first appeared. This editor agrees with the magazine editors who thought they should. These are *not* sequences of haiku or senryu—very few of the lines could stand alone as poems—but taken in context they give the kinds of effects those genres do. They present moments of awareness of both nature and human nature, and each keeps the breath-long form of those genres. Their roots are haiku and senryu but *they* are something new, and until they were written there was nothing in English quite like them. Longer forms like this allow the haiku or senryu poet to explore experience more fully—not only "moments" but the duration of time and the phenomenon of memory.

Though they are something new, they do have precedents in Japanese literary history, as does the dissenting critic's objection mentioned above. Sequences of haiku called *rensaku* have usually been written with haiku that can stand alone, but some poets have written rensaku in which the parts can only function as haiku within the context of the sequence, and they have been criticized for it.*

* See Donald Keene's *Dawn to the West: Japanese Literature in the Modern Era; Poetry, Drama, Criticism*, pp. 143-144.

"SEQUENCES"   BY MARLENE MOUNTAIN

sequence : one

you cup my breasts i tablespoon you
      a late monarch   your fingers slowly find my folds
your kiss on my cloud mountain   moonrise
      mountain tip from mist my clitoris rises to your mouth
the maple just turning i fill my mouth with you
      your sawedoff thumb deep deeper beyond my moon
new moon   you find the blood between us
      i rise from blood and paint myself in the moon
i am my reason for living your love in the falling leaves
      mountain   just the tip of me
as you leave i remain a mountain of folds

sequence : two

clothed-naked we begin passion already in our laughter
      our hands together we part over each other
as we touch i know myself in your closed eyes
      your voice disappears into a poem on my walls

sequence : three

in winter rain we kiss dry my suitcase closed
      car trouble the distance from you farther
the day ends a borrowed sleeping bag on a stained mattress
      a poem not yet formed festering
small bottle of gin in another town someone's ice cubes
      a party two states from home i just get high
morning news i switch to country music and think of sex
      busboy unaware of the yolk
no card in the motel lobby says it
      the key turned in: returning
a week of theater continues an off-size sunday flat
      first mountain: to hump or to be humped
is it you or the mountain i am wet in my jeans
      unpacked in the mountain fold alone

sequence : four
your hand on me you read about yourself in a poem
          we share a gin shoes touching
you harden march blows through the partly opened window
          one stick we float in and out of love
high   giggling about giggling between orgasms
          i come to know your fingers
spring wind in the night my breasts reshaped
          morning we wash ourselves onto each other
after you've gone you reappear in the sound of rain

sequence : five   (sono mama: things as they are)
i am here you there first night of spring
          the sun rose before i woke
ground uncovered asparagus appear when they appear
          nothing in the mail
the canvas ready swollen buds
          my painting surprises me
march a month not unlike my life
          night air drops again
one kind of poverty one kind of poem
          having bloomed the daffodil

sequence : six
the parting and the returning first leaves of the hepatica
          the bloom begins the touch of your eyes
in the darkness with you there is no darkness with you
          night i ride in clouds beneath the faded roof
together as we dry there is the listening to rain
          steam of morning coffee the lingering
after the long party we love as the wine allows
          your last breakfast: i catch a rainbow
deep within your breathing the leaving of tomorrow
          the silence left by your truck on the blacktop

sequence : seven   (through the moon)
to and from: the tractor a neighbor's garden
            the moon comes full you fill me
late afternoon the hoer puts away the hoe
            the wait: the moon to darken red
on a stake a beet packet rattles in the wind
            your voice from a distant pay phone
phoebe phoebe phoebe phoebe the days you're gone
            quarter phase i touch my stomach
first two leaves
            rain: fifty fifty
alone in bed i write a poem alone
            in the white of the painting
dogwood only the emptiness in bloom
            you return and come
awakened by your touch awake to your touch
            wrinkled clothes in another room
a truck driver waves spring morning
            Y: we part
in your leaving there is yesterday and tomorrow
            new moon: ishtar and i redden together
before the ink is dry your lips
            beneath stars one nipple cold
you dowse the fire heavy dew stirring me
            facing the wooden wall receiving
already the quarter already the halving

sequence : eight

in the old turtle shell you give love in the evening
        thunderhead the unthinking of our passion
afternoon warmth the puddle swarming with tadpoles
        spring peepers you too are male
do you know: mozart's "magic flute"
        to what depth do we play
even in the nibble of minnows there is fishing
        your hand under your shirt finds me
easier to let go knowing you're stuck on me
        last touch hand on the cold doorknob
the old shirt you gave me on the hanger you forgot
        i almost write nothing in my journal
one poem—half my life through this portable
        tonight i am mountain
unviewed the moon rises in one of her phases
        alone the nipplelessness of nipples
broad daylight bareassed insects mating in flight
        swifts foreplay the chimney
forest fire in the next county will i again be burned
        mist

sequence : nine

there is art there is beer on another mountain
        you across the long narrow state
route one in the mountains in the moon
        home again the bare mattress enough
there is art there is beer on this mountain
        you across the long narrow state

III: Criticism and a Sequence

There are four examples of criticism in this section. Two are reviews of a small chapbook by John Wills, one of the haiku movement's most accomplished poets. The other two concern the work of Alexis Rotella: Rod Willmot's introduction to one of her chapbooks, and a review by Marlene Mountain of that book and one other by the same author. Both Mountain and Willmot refer to the poems they discuss as "haiku." Though Rotella has written many fine haiku—several are included in this anthology—the work she is best known for, and which is primarily being discussed in these critical pieces, should be called "serious senryu." Willmot has, elsewhere, called this type of poem "psychological haiku." Aside from this, the editor is in agreement with just about everything these poet/critics have to say in praise of Rotella's work. Her sequence *After an Affair* is included here rather than elsewhere in the anthology because Mountain's review makes an excellent introduction to it.

A Troutswirl Simplicity

Up a Distant Ridge
31 haiku by John Wills
2¼ in. high x 8½ in. wide, 36 pages
The First Haiku Press, Manchester, NH. 1980. $1.00.

Simplify! simplify! simplify! said J. W. Hackett more than fifteen years ago. He was applying Thoreau's admonition on how to live to the writing of haiku. And a number of American haiku poets have been following that advice diligently in the intervening years. It's hard to imagine anyone taking simplicity much further than John Wills has in his latest book *Up a Distant Ridge*, a matchless collection of 31 one-line haiku,* almost all with the simplicity of form, language, and image of a swirl of water in a stream.

> dusk   from rock to rock a waterthrush

For me these nine syllables—almost like a jotted notation in a pocket diary—call into being the things named in such a way that a whole mountain-forest environment rises up with them. In the shadows beyond the rocks, about which the dull glitter of the stream's last light swirls into foam, the heavy foliage of trees darkly fades up into the walls of a ravine. The bird moves about in a deepening solitude. Its movement reflects, helps to call into image, into being, the movement of the stream, whose waters are simply evoked by the bird's name. The bird moves in mystery—for at dusk, which somehow is *the* time to bring out the nature, the essence, of a waterthrush, it is hard to be sure if it is flying, hopping, or even going under water, like a water ouzel, as it appears first here, then there, as if by magic.

The harsh, stark "k" sounds of the words for the surrounding "inanimate" features of the landscape—dusk and rock—contrast and help to isolate the relative softness of the word "waterthrush," the only spot of life in the gathering darkness. Yet the iambic flow of the line, combined with the bird's movements, draws everything together into a unity where the bird is not alone at all, but is one with rock, water, and dusk—one with the universe—and we are too.

> rain in gusts   below the deadhead troutswirl

To experience this haiku's full resonance one should be aware of the several states, or conditions, of water that precede and accompany the moment of the troutswirl. For its few words call up not only "rain in gusts" but, by suggestion, the steadier fall

---

* Wills later made all but a few of these haiku into three-liners—in most cases without changing a word. Some were originally written in three lines. Wills' haiku are so concise, they often work both ways.

of rain, or mistiness, or even absence of rain, which comes between the gusts, the flowing, swelling sweep of the water of the stream, or river, above the deadhead (a wholly or partly sunken log) as it tries to get around the obstruction, the smoothness of the quiet water just below it, the meeting of the three or four kinds of rain on the different kinds of river surface, and finally the troutswirl itself. The many images of water united in one. And out of this elemental world of river, wind, and rain—and "death"—comes that one sign of life. As in the "waterthrush" haiku, the mystery is deepened as much by what we don't see as by what we do, for the trout itself is either unseen, or just barely glimpsed through the water.

Here is one more word-spell from the book:

the sun lights up a distant ridge   another

The power that John Wills has packed into that one word "another" is one of the most amazing acts of compression since God crammed e into mc^2. For look, inside it is another ridge being lit up, and then another, and another . . . and on to some lost horizon of the infinite.

Compare this to an earlier haiku by Wills (from *Back Country*, 1969):

the hills
  release the summer clouds
    one . . . by one . . . by one . . .

This is a marvelous haiku too, but look at the advance Wills has made in simplicity and depth with the later one. It is not only the single line, or the fewer words, or fewer syllables . . . but it is the sureness of phrase, the restraint, the rightness in that final word, and the feeling that a master has found out a secret of language and existence so that finally the simple, ordinary, abstract word "another" has come to glory.

—Cor van den Heuvel
in *Frogpond* IV, 4 (1981)

John Wills' *Up a Distant Ridge* comes in an unattractive edition, bookmark-shaped and poorly reproduced. But I would rather have the thirty-one haiku here than many a thicker, more luxurious volume. These are poems of very great depth; beyond their technical perfection, they demonstrate that acute observation of suchnesses is not enough, that there must be a sense of the man behind the work, the shaping personality that has itself been shaped by experience. Here are three, to begin with (all one-liners):

below the falls a boat slides under willows
parka in the morning drizzle fishing
pines absorb the fussing of the titmice

In the first poem the parallel of falls and willows creates a gentle, dream-like quality (like the letting-down of a woman's hair) in which the boat seems almost to seek refuge. In the second poem the refuge (the parka) is like a shell, whose inhabitant—the poet himself?—is completely hidden; yet a fishing-rod protrudes like an antenna, a continuance of human activity. In the third poem the sheltering is externalized; the "fussing" may be only the small, quick movements of feeding birds, yet the word connotes disquiet. And although all that really happens (perhaps) is that the birds move off through the forest, in the poet's vision there has been a calming, an absorption of disquiet by a life-form larger than ourselves.

rain in gusts   below the deadhead troutswirl
slats of the neighbor's broken fence   striped cushaws
a mourning cloak sailing down the deerpath

The complexity of the first poem begins with the gusts and troutswirl, whose motion is similar. An opposition, or equivalence? With Wills the activity of fishing is one of communion, not competition; the fishing-line permits contact, not exploitation. And it seems that standing in the gusting rain, for Wills, is also an act of communion, as though the poet were a sort of fish in the weather's water. If the beginning and end of the poem reflect one another, both being in a sense "life-signs," they are together opposed (with Wills) to the waterlogged "death-sign" between them: the deadhead. In the second poem a still more innocent scene bears similar implications. Cushaws (the stress is on the second syllable) are a type of squash with a long, curved neck. Their striping is reflected in the slatted fence, but the rest is unmistakable opposition: between that which is rectangular, thin, broken, *inanimate,* and that which is rounded, whole, *alive.* The most striking expression of this theme, however, is in the final poem. Here a butterfly whose very name conjures up death embodies that astonishing combination of vulnerability and bravado that is of the essence of living. And at the heart of poetry. All in all—and much more could be said—this is a most substantial collection.

—Rod Willmot
in *Cicada* 4, 3 (1980)

During the 1970s haiku came of age in North America, largely due to a small vanguard of poets who refined the form to the limits of concision. They carried the haiku movement forward to the point where we are now secure in writing much more laconically—and effectively—than we used to. It seems that in the 1980s there is a new focus of experimentation, dealing with content rather than form. The vanguard now is a scattered handful of poets—Alexis Rotella among them—in whose work the full intensity of haiku perception is turned upon the human condition.

On a White Bud celebrates the intimately dangerous awareness of being alive, of being, even in pain, exquisitely human:

> Vase of peonies:
> on a white bud
> lipstick print

The formerly "pure" world of Nature is now imprinted with human presence, and in the imprint chosen we read everything a kiss might be, every service the lips might fulfill. We read ourselves: our grace in giving, our innocence in accepting nourishment, our pursuit of love, our sharing of speech with each other.

These poems offer surprisingly varied insights into human experience. Relationships predominate, but of many kinds and as seen from many angles. Friend, lover, husband, father, mother, grandmother . . . children and the dead are evoked as well. There is an undercurrent of poignancy, in that so often the poem occurs precisely at the junction of contact and separation:

Phone call
his three-day stubble
scraping the distance

Discussing divorce
he strokes
the lace tablecloth

In each of these haiku the Other communicates least through his intentions, most through some unintended or absent-minded act that ever so briefly eradicates distance.

Of all the qualities of Alexis Rotella's haiku, two in particular contribute to my enjoyment of this collection: a sense of the poet's vulnerability, and the unfailing awareness that she is a woman. To cry out in an empty room, to seek comfort where none may be had, to confess one's yearning even as one escapes it momentarily—these are hard in themselves, but it is harder still to permit ourselves to be aware of them. It takes strength to be vulnerable. Yet allowing oneself to do so confers even greater strength in return, and the same can be said of writing from the sensibility of one's sex. It is so much easier and safer to write from a neuter perspective, a pair of eyes with whatever is behind them carefully veiled. In expressing herself so completely as a woman, Alexis Rotella comes before us without armor, so to speak, yet with a power whose source is old and very deep. To read these poems is to know that one has received a rich and nourishing gift:

Late August
I bring him the garden
in my skirt

—Rod Willmot, 1983

REVIEW OF *On a White Bud* AND *After an Affair*
BY ALEXIS ROTELLA

There was a time we knew next to nothing about our fellow poets, not from their haiku at least, other than some practiced zazen, took canoe trips, watched birds, and so on. More recently, however, we've found that there are poets who actually get angry, have troubles and conflicts, occasionally make love, and even have an affair. No longer just silhouettes and shadows in our poems, we've begun to take on flesh; no longer mere observers of phenomena, we *are* the phenomena.

As Rod Wilmot, in his introduction to Alexis Rotella's *On a White Bud,* so aptly says: "The formerly 'pure' world of Nature is now imprinted with human presence." Rotella, indeed, allows us into her personal world

Discussing divorce
he strokes
the lace tablecloth

In the guest room
where my mother slept
I look for comfort

I found myself caught up in particular by the various mentions of he/him/his. Rotella is at times listening to and quarrelling with him, watching him and holding his gaze, missing him, trying to forget him, and crying out after he leaves. One man? Two?

Only I laugh
at his joke . .
the silence

Left to the wind
all the lilies
and all his lies

I began to want to know who is who and which is which, yet to the end remained confused by the lack of definition.

Along with the fine haiku, there are times when Rotella lets us in and there is nothing there

> Arranging tea roses Alone
> I watch him climb in the Chinese restaurant,
> the ladder dropping a chopstick

Or if there is meaning it is well hidden, i.e., a poem is not set well enough in context to allow the mood or information from surrounding haiku to assist it (thereby enabling it to exist with less). And there are of course, as with all of us, some poems over which to groan. Yet as there are many snags when truly trout fishing, similarly there are bound to be snags when writing about ourselves, our fears, our loneliness, our pains. Perhaps though, in that we do write (in that we do try), we, in one way, do succeed. Or to say it another way, it is perhaps from our failed haiku we learn we were not quite open or honest and are haunted until we get deeper into ourselves—and get it right.

With these feelings about Rotella's writing in mind, I was quite unprepared for her latest book. *After an Affair* blew me away. I was deeply moved—something I rarely experience in haiku. Everything came into place. What seems "almost" in *Bud* truly flowers in *After an Affair*. What, in *Bud,* seems puzzling or maybe none of my business, in *Affair,* calls out and takes me in. I experience with Rotella the stuff of life—and happily the stuff of art. Whereas *Bud* is a collection of haiku, *Affair* is a sequence of living. I feel so strongly that it is a sequence in which one haiku deepens as it follows and co-exists with others, that I'd rather not quote from it. The poems belong together to be experienced together.

More and more, as I flounder through my own days and nights, I want to know how my companion travelers do it, survive this crazy desperate thing we call life on the planet. I take heart I am not the only one who wants to share, nor the only one who wants to know

> deep autumn my neighbor what does she do
> *Bashō*

—Marlene Mountain
in *Frogpond* VII, 3 (1984)

Song-sparrow:
I awake from a dream
still a young woman

Wild touch-me-nots:
you never
touch me

The peace-lily opens:
still this rift
between us

Garden tilled:
we speak
of separating

Sipping wine:
I remember your face
the way it used to be

Mourning doves:
they cry just loud
and long enough

The butterfly
from last night's dream
waiting on the mailbox

Just friends:
he watches my gauze dress
blowing on the line

Not yet lovers
we drink
from the same cup

As we enter
the hot room,
scent of peaches

After watermelon
shivering
in his arms

A moth touches
the pink clover
then leaves

After he leaves
the cobwebs
in the stairwell

Love seat:
straightening
the doilie

After an affair
sweeping
all the rooms

A white lie
growing bigger:
mock orange

During our little talk
I tear a daisy
to shreds

As we quarrel
my breasts
aching

Summer breeze:
a letter
from his wife

During my grief
the sound of a neighbor
sweeping her walk

You bring me tea
as if everything
were perfect

—Alexis Rotella

APPENDIX B: DEFINITIONS

The following are newly revised definitions. They are based on definitions prepared for the Haiku Society of America in 1973 by Harold G. Henderson, William J. Higginson, and Anita Virgil, and which appeared in the first edition of this book. Incorporated into them are emendations concerning the meaning of the word *onji* which were suggested by Tadashi Kondo in the society's magazine *Frogpond* (I, 4, 1978). The editor of this book has made significant changes and additions, so the following are not necessarily the opinions of any of the above-named persons or the HSA.

PRELIMINARY NOTE

1. The Japanese word *onji* (sound-symbol) has been mistranslated into English as "syllable" for many years. However, in most Japanese poetry the *onji* does not correspond to the Western notion of syllable. For example, while each of the words "hokku" and "haiku" is reckoned as two syllables in English, they are each counted as three *onji* in Japanese, and "senryu" is counted as four. Also, where each Japanese *onji* is equal and brief as "do, re, mi, etc.," English single syllables can vary greatly in time duration.
2. Each of the words defined is its own plural.

Haiku

(1) An unrhymed Japanese poem recording the essence of a moment keenly perceived in which nature is linked to human nature. It usually consists of 17 *onji* (Japanese sound-symbols) in three parts of 5-7-5 *onji* each.
(2) An adaptation in English of (1) usually written in one to three lines with no specific number of syllables. It rarely has more than 17 syllables. Sometimes written in three lines of 5, 7, and 5 syllables each.

Though in the past English language haiku were often written in three lines of 5, 7, and 5 syllables each, most are now written in a free-verse form of fewer than 17 syllables. This comes closer to the Japanese "form" because 10 to 14 syllables in English approximate the spoken length of 17 *onji* in Japanese. Even in Japanese haiku is not a "form" in the same sense that a sonnet or triolet is a "form" in English. This is demonstrated by the fact that the Japanese differentiate haiku from senryu—a type of poem that has exactly the same "form" as haiku but differs in content from it. Actually, there is no rigid form for Japanese haiku. Seventeen *onji* is the norm, but some 5 percent of "classical" haiku depart from it, and so do a still greater percentage of modern Japanese haiku. To the Japanese and to English language haiku poets, it is the content and not the form alone that makes a haiku. That content is nature. All Japanese classical haiku, as well as most modern ones, contain *a kigo* (season-word: a word that indicates a season of the year*) which ensures that nature will be in the poem; senryu do not. While there is no season-word tradition or rule in English language haiku, a season if not expressly indicated is usually felt or implied. Nature in some sense must be present, and in some particular object—not generalized or allegorized. Haiku poets may find it in some unlikely places, however. Nature can be found on city streets as well as in the woods. It is wherever there is light or darkness, sound or silence, heat or cold—in whatever can be seen, heard, smelled, or touched. Haiku relates us to nature through the senses. "Coming to one's senses" in haiku means seeing things as they are, realizing reality as it is—seeing one thing so clearly, we see the oneness of all things.

---

* For example, "frog" indicates spring, "lightning" indicates summer. A detailed examination of the use of *kigo* and a sample season-word list may be found in William J. Higginson's *The Haiku Handbook*.

Hokku
(1) The first stanza of a Japanese linked-verse poem (see *Haikai no renga*).
(2) (Obsolete) A haiku.

Senryu
(1) A Japanese poem with the same form as the haiku but concerned with human nature and human relationships. It is usually humorous or satiric.
(2) An adaptation in English of (1) with the same form as the English language haiku. English language senryu can be serious, humorous, or a mixture of both.

Haikai no renga
A type of Japanese linked-verse poem, popular from the fifteenth through the nineteenth centuries. *Haikai no renga* normally consist of 36, 50, or 100 stanzas, alternating 17 and 14 *onji*. Usually a small group of poets took turns composing the stanzas, whose content and grammar were governed by fairly complex rules.

Renga
An adaptation in English of the Japanese *haikai no renga*. It is usually written in 36 stanzas or less, alternating 3- and 2-line stanzas of no specific syllable length.

In Japanese the word *haikai* is commonly used as an abbreviation for *haikai no renga,* usually translated as "comic linked-verse." Under the influence of Bashō (1644–1694) the tone of *haikai no renga* became more serious but the name was retained. The haiku developed from the hokku, the first stanza of a *haikai no renga*.

The word *haikai* is also used in Japanese as a general term for all haiku-related literature (haiku, *haikai no renga,* the diaries of haiku poets, etc.). In Spanish and French the word *haikai* is often used to refer to either the Japanese haiku or Western adaptations of the form. However, in modern Japanese usage reference to a single *haikai* is to a *haikai no renga*.

Haibun

(1) A Japanese prose piece by a haiku poet written in an elliptical and pithy style and in the spirit of haiku. It usually includes one or more haiku, and can be in length from a short sketch to a book-length diary.
(2) An adaptation in English of (1).

APPENDIX C: BIOGRAPHICAL NOTES

The following brief biographical entries include the state, province, or country where the poet currently resides, date and place of birth, and most recent book. For addresses of the haiku presses—Burnt Lake, From Here, High/Coo, and Wind Chimes—see the Book List that follows the Preface.

Helen C. Acton: Oregon; 11/27/1913 Volin, SD.

Eric Amann: Ontario; 1938 Munich, Germany; *Cicada Voices: Selected Haiku of Eric Amann 1966–1979*, edited by George Swede, High/Coo Press, 1983.

Nick Avis: Newfoundland; 1/7/1957 London, England; *Abandoned Outport*, self-published, 1984.

Bob Boldman: Ohio; 6/22/1950 Dayton, OH; *Heart and Bones*, Wind Chimes Press, 1985.

Janice Bostok: Australia; 4/9/1942 Mullumbimby, New South Wales; *On Sparse Bush*, Makar Press (University of Queensland), Brisbane, Queensland, 1978 (No. 29 Gargoyle Poets Series).

Chuck Brickley: British Columbia; 10/11/1947 San Francisco; *Earthshine*, an unpublished sequence.

Martin Burke: New York, 7/28/1941 New York City.

Jack Cain: Ontario; 12/16/1940 Newmarket, Ontario; *Two Brown Ducks*, unpublished.

Gerard John Conforti: New York; 2/26/1948 New York.

Richard Crist: last resided New York; 11/1/1909 Cleveland, OH (d. 1985); *The Queekup Spring* (children's story), Abelard-Schuman, 1961.

L. A. Davidson: New York; 7/31/1917 on a ranch near Roy, MT; *The Shape of the Tree*, Wind Chimes Press, 1982.

Betty Drevniok: Ontario; 12/17/1919 St. Louis, MO; *Aware: A Haiku Primer*, Portal Publications, Bellingham, WA, 1980.

Michael Dudley: Ontario; 6/2/1953 Toronto, Ontario; *A Man in a Motel Room*, forthcoming in 1986 from High/Coo Press.

Larry Gates: Mississippi; 6/12/1942 Chicago, IL.

LeRoy Gorman: Ontario; 8/7/1949 Smith Falls, Ontario; *beautiful chance*, South Western Ontario Poetry, 1984.

Rosamond Haas: Michigan; 7/1/1908 Kalamazoo, MI; *North Portal*, E. P. Dutton, New York, 1957.

J. W. Hackett: California; 8/6/1929 Seattle, WA; *The Zen Haiku and Other Zen Poems of J. W. Hackett*, Japan Publications, Tokyo, 1983 (see Book List following Preface).

Jim Handlin: New Jersey; 11/14/1943 Boston, MA; *The Distance in a Door*, Gusto Press, New York, 1981.

Lorraine Ellis Harr: Oregon; 10/31/— Sullivan, IL; *Seventy-Sevens: Sequence of Haiku*, Middlewood Press, Magna, UT.

Penny Harter: New Jersey; 4/9/1940 New York City; *In the Broken Curve*, Burnt Lake Press, 1984.

William J. Higginson: New Jersey; 12/17/1938 New York City; *The Haiku*

Handbook: How to Write, Share, and Teach Haiku, McGraw-Hill, New York, 1985.

Gary Hotham: A.P.O. New York (Germany); 7/28/1950 Presque Isle, ME; *This Space Blank,* Juniper Press, La Crosse, WI, 1984.

Clement Hoyt: last resided Texas; 5/14/1906 Houston, TX (d. 1970); *Storm of Stars,* The Green World, Baton Rouge, LA, 1976.

Foster Jewell: last resided Illinois; 7/21/1893 Grand Rapids, MI (d. 1984); *Exhaling Green,* Sangre de Cristo Press, Venice, CA, 1980.

Jack Kerouac: last resided Florida; 1922 Lowell, MA (d. 1969); *Scattered Poems,* City Lights Books, San Francisco, 1971.

Gustave Keyser: last resided Texas; 2/19/1910 place? (d. 1978).

Tadashi Kondo: Japan; 3/30/1949 Miyazaki, Japan; *Twelve Tokyo Renga 1980–1982,* with Kris Young, Robert Reed, Philip Meredith, and others, forthcoming from From Here Press.

Elizabeth Searle Lamb: New Mexico; 1/22/1917 Topeka, KA; *Casting Into a Cloud: Southwest Haiku,* From Here Press, 1985.

Ruth Latta: North Carolina; 12/2/1900 Buffalo, NY; *Dandelions,* J & C Transcripts, Kanona, NY, 1978.

David E. LeCount: California; 8/10/1944 place? *Gaining Amber,* Brussels Sprout Press, Mountain Lakes, NJ, 1981.

Geraldine Clinton Little: New Jersey; 9/20/— Portstewart, Ireland; *Endless Waves,* Merging Media, Westfield, NJ, 1984.

David Lloyd: New Jersey; 5/9/1930 Montclair, NJ; *Snowman,* haiku and illustrations by David Lloyd, The Rook Press, P.O.B. 144, Ruffsdale, PA 15679, 1978.

Peggy Lyles: Georgia; 9/17/1939 Summerville, SC; *Still at the Edge,* Swamp Press, Oneonta, NY, 1980.

Matsuo Allard (also known as R. Clarence Matsuo-Allard): last known address in New Hampshire; c. 1949? New Hampshire? *Bird Day Afternoon,* High/Coo Press, 1978.

Michael McClintock: California; 3/31/1950 Los Angeles; *Maya: Poems 1968–1975,* Seer Ox, Los Angeles, 1976.

Scott Montgomery: Massachusetts; 5/30/51 Ithaca, NY.

Lenard D. Moore: North Carolina; 2/13/1958 Jacksonville, NC; *The Open Eye,* North Carolina Haiku Society Press, 1985.

Marlene Mountain (also known as Marlene Wills): Tennessee; 12/11/1939 Ada, OK; *tonight i am mountain: the haiku sequences,* forthcoming from Burnt Lake Press.

Alan Pizzarelli: New Jersey; 1/12/1950 Newark, NJ; *Frozen Socks,* forthcoming from Pizzazz Publications, Newark.

Claire Pratt: Ontario; 3/21/1918 Toronto, Ontario; *The Music of Oberon,* Art Press, CT, 1975.

Marjory Bates Pratt: New Jersey; 6/16/1896 Waterville, ME; *The Light on the Snow,* lettered, reproduced, and bound by the author, 1979.

Frank K. Robinson: Tennessee; 11/11/1931 Lamesa, TX.

Emily Romano: New Jersey; 12/28/1924 Boonton, NJ; *Pear Blossoms Drift,* High/Coo Press, 1981.

Raymond Roseliep: last resided Iowa; 8/11/1917 Farley, IA (d. 1983); *The*

Earth We Swing On, photos by Cyril A. Reilly and Renée Travis Reilly; Winston Press, Minneapolis, MN, 1984.

Sydell Rosenberg: New York: 12/15/1929 New York City.

Alexis Rotella: New Jersey, 1/16/1947 Johnstown, PA; *Middle City: Regional Poems & Haiku,* Muse Pie Press, Passaic, NJ, 1986.

Hal Roth: Maryland; 4/13/31 Northampton, PA; *Touching the Stone Ax,* Wind Chimes Press, 1984.

Hiroaki Sato: New York; 3/21/1942 Japan; *The Sword and the Mind,* Overlook Press, 1986.

Myra Scovel: New York; 8/11/1905 Mechanicville, NY; *In Clover* (prose), Westminster Press, Philadelphia, 1980.

Michael Segers: Georgia; 7/10/1950 Macon, GA.

Martin Shea: California; 7/1/1941 New York City; *blackdog in the headlights,* Shelters Press, Milwaukee, WI, 1975.

O. Mabson Southard (also known as Mabelsson Norway): *Marsh-grasses,* American Haiku Press, Platteville, WI, 1967.

Robert Spiess: Wisconsin; 10/16/1921 Milwaukee, WI; *The Bold Silverfish and Tall River Junction,* forthcoming in 1986 from Modern Haiku, Madison, WI.

George Swede: Ontario; 11/20/1940 Riga, Latvia; *High Wire Spider,* Three Trees Press, Toronto, Ontario, 1986.

Tom Tico: California; 5/15/1942 San Francisco.

James Tipton: Colorado; 1/18/1942 Ashland, OH; *The Third Coast: Contemporary Michigan Fiction,* Wayne State University Press, 1976.

Cor van den Heuvel: New York; 3/6/1931 Biddeford, ME; *Dark,* Chant Press, New York, 1982.

Anita Virgil: New Jersey; 11/23/1931 Baltimore, MD; *A 2nd Flake,* Montclair, NJ.

Nicholas Virgilio: 1092 Niagara Road, Camden, New Jersey; 6/28/1928 Camden, NJ; *Selected Haiku,* Burnt Lake Press, 1985.

Larry Wiggin: last resided New Hampshire; 11/15/1919 Northfield, NH (d. 1973); *loose kites,* self-published broadside, 1973.

Rod Willmot: Quebec; 12/27/1948 Toronto, Ontario; *The Ribs of Dragonfly,* Black Moss Press, Windsor, Ontario, 1985.

John Wills: Florida; 7/4/1921 Los Angeles; *Up a Distant Ridge,* First Haiku Press, Manchester, NH, 1980.

Ruth Yarrow: New York; 9/15/1939 Camden, NJ; *Down Marble Canyon,* Wind Chimes Press, 1984.

Kenneth Yasuda: Indiana; 6/23/1914 Auburn, CA; *The Japanese Haiku,* Charles E. Tuttle Co., Rutland, VT, and Tokyo, 1957.

Virginia Brady Young: Connecticut; 12/2/1918 New York City; *Waterfall,* Timberline Press, Fulton, MO, 1984.

Arizona Zipper: Maine; born in the White Mountains.

364